"The Magical Path is a great ro
frequented by many great na
MacGregor Mathers, Dion Fortune, Helena Раιrоνнα
Blavatsky, Eliphas Levi, to name but a few. You will find
their footprints along the way. It is my hope that this
volume will encourage you to find your own path so that
you may open up a road not previously charted."

—Gerald del Campo

Finding your own individual path is the most challeng-
ing journey any of us takes. What oath to take? What
discipline to practice? What creed to swear by? The
choices today are innumerable yet simultaneously overwhelming in their abundance. After embarking on this
journey himself, Ordo Templi Orientis Quartermaster
and ordained Ecclesia Gnostica Catholica priest Gerald
del Campo created a simple but magnificent travel assis-
tant called *New Aeon Magick*. It is a clear and engaging
guide to deciphering the many possible New Aeon paths
before you. The beauty, significance and method of the
art of magical living is presented in a down-to-earth style
free from the arrogance that marks so many manuals on
the esoteric.

Whether your path leads you to environmental
awareness, higher consciousness, greater tolerance, or
the attainment of an inner balance does not matter.
What *New Aeon Magick* encourages is a magical curriculum that, through your investment of action and energy,
is uniquely yours, allowing you to be who you are and,
ultimately, affecting the world through your own vitally
personal magical link.

About the Author

Gerald del Campo was born in Cordoba, Argentina, on January 14, 1960. He is a member and Master of his own Oasis chartered by the Ordo Templi Orientis (O.T.O.), a magical/philosophical Order made known to the English-speaking nations by Aleister Crowley during the Victorian era. Del Campo has also maintained previous membership with two other groups that have strong claims of succession from the Hermetic Order of the Golden Dawn. He publishes a bimonthly newsletter, *The Rpstoval Review,* and presently writes for an O.T.O. publication called *The Baphomet Breeze.*

To Write to the Author

If you wish to contact the author or would like more information about this book, please write to the author in care of Llewellyn Worldwide and we will forward your request. Both the author and publisher appreciate hearing from you and learning of your enjoyment of this book and how it has helped you. Llewellyn Worldwide cannot guarantee that every letter written to the author can be answered, but all will be forwarded. Please write to:

Gerald del Campo
c/o Llewellyn Worldwide
P.O. Box 64383-439, St. Paul, MN 55164-0383, U.S.A.

Please enclose a self-addressed, stamped envelope for reply, or $1.00
to cover costs.
If outside U.S.A., enclose international postal reply coupon.

Free Catalog from Llewellyn

For more than 90 years Llewellyn has brought its readers knowledge in the fields of metaphysics and human potential. Learn about the newest books in spiritual guidance, natural healing, astrology, occult philosophy and more. Enjoy book reviews, new age articles, a calendar of events, plus current advertised products and services. To get your free copy of *Llewellyn's New Worlds of Mind and Spirit,* send your name and address to:

Llewellyn's New Worlds of Mind and Spirit
P.O. Box 64383-439, St. Paul, MN 55164-0383, U.S.A.

NEW
AEON MAGICK

Thelema Without Tears

Gerald del Campo

1994
Llewellyn Publications
St. Paul, Minnesota 55164–0383, U.S.A.

FIRST EDITION
First Printing, 1994

Library of Congress Cataloging in Publication Data

Del Campo, Gerald, 1960–
    New aeon magick : thelema without tears / Gerald del Campo.
      p. cm.
    ISBN 1–56718–213–5 (soft) : $9.99 ($13.50 Can.)
    1. Magic. 2. Ritual. I. Title. II. Title: Thelema without
tears.
    BF1611.D35   1994
    133.4'3—dc20   94–15748
                                                      CIP

Llewellyn Publications
A Division of Llewellyn Worldwide, Ltd.
P.O. Box 64383, St. Paul, MN 55164-0383

To my three children:
Christopher, Donathan, and Samantha.

May you reach heights I have only dreamt about.

I'd like to thank my mom Olga, my dad Henry, and my sister Gabie. Also, Jim Eshelman, Anna'Kria King, Phyllis Seckler; David, Lynn, Lexy and Luscha Scriven, Hymenaeus Beta, Bill Heidrick, David Kennedy, April Norton, Lon Milo DuQuette; Craig, Laurie, and Lenore Berry, Vere Chappel, Michelle Spadotto, Scott Fineberg, Caryle Lasman, Steve Hedrick, Kayla Block, Doug and Karen James, the Ordo Templi Orientis, the Temple of Thelema, the College of Thelema, the Fraternitas LVX Occulta, Paul and Linda Clark, Frater Quartus Kerub, Rusty Sporer; Joe, Sophia and William Larabell, Mark Garrison, Darrin Hyrup, Daniel Hammock and Shyla Butler, Julie Weber, Mitch Ansteine, Rena Schlossnagel, Laura Cannon, Michael Glosson, and all my friends at Baphomet Lodge in Hollywood, whom without their friendship and support this book could never have happened. And a very special thanks to Monique, my wife, who stood by me during the laughter and the tears, and insisted that I write a longer book than I really wanted to. And a special heart felt thanks to the Spirit of Richard McGrew who still keeps us all warm in the cold winter months.

Table of Contents

Illustrations

Introduction

Do what thou wilt shall be the whole of the Law.

Magick may be described as a system of communication, a language used exclusively between the conscious (the logical mind) and the subconscious (the thinking mind). During dialogue, the magician's objective is to use his or her logical mind to convince the thinking mind to reveal a method by which to directly access the superconscious, the higher mind … the Holy Guardian Angel.

Every 2,000 years or so we enter into a new age. At this time, the subconscious changes, and so does the language to which it responds. Once this shift has occurred, the magician must make the necessary adjustments if he wants to keep the dialogue open. Should you fall into the rut called "tradition"(as many magicians do) you will no longer be able to affect those subtle forces which you are trying to stimulate because you will not understand them.

In 1904 we entered such an age. The angel Aiwass announced that Horus, the hawk-headed god, had taken his seat at the Throne of the Gods. The Aeon of the Child was upon us. As with most children, this one naturally has a rebellious attitude towards the old ways, and it insists on creating new ways of doing things. The New Aeon brought with it a new law: **"Do what thou wilt shall be the whole of the Law,"** and **"Love is the law, love under will."** This unprecedented law demands the utmost discipline. It suggests that we all have a purpose, a will; and that we have a responsibility to follow that will, to live in harmony with the rest of the universe, and to be who we truly are.

By virtue of this law, not only are we freed from the bonds of ignorance which the previous aeon brought, but it is emphasized that we protect our originality. The magical formula for the New Aeon must be structured in such a way that it can be distinguished from the old formulae, yet it must be capable of overwhelming tolerance in order to allow great diversity.

The purpose of this book is to help you to discover the new language by which to communicate with your Self. This will help you to further understand the books already on your shelves, and most importantly; it will give you a foundation on which to create your own unique methods. These methods will work better than anything learned from any book because you created them for yourself. Although one will find ritual and instruction in this book, it is presented solely for the purpose of presenting the reader with some effective procedures. It is my hope that you will familiarize yourself with the mechanics involved in ceremonial magick, thereby becoming fit to design your own rituals.

Originally, I wrote this book for my three children, and for that reason you will find that I have written it in the "second person"; I hope this informality does not offend anyone. The purpose of this little work is not to show great literary skill, but rather to shed light on a difficult subject further made obscure by authors looking for scholarly recognition. This limited volume does not contain "all that there is." No one could boast about having written such a book. You should simply view this as a primer.

The only thing that I ask is that you keep a diary. This will serve you by creating a "book of spells," a reference that you can review to chart your progress along the Path. It will also serve those that come after you by providing them with insight about an otherwise unknown approach. No matter how swiftly you have progressed, if you have left nothing to the next generation of magicians, then your contribution to the Great Work will have been limited to its evolutionary representation.

The magical path is a great road to travel; it has been frequented by many great names: Aleister Crowley, MacGregor Mathers, Dion Fortune, Helena Patrovna Blavatsky, Eliphas Levi, to name but a few. You will see their footprints along the way. It is my hope that this volume will encourage you to find your own path, so that you may open up a road not previously charted.

Love is the law, love under will.

GERALD DEL CAMPO

March 21, 1993
Ashland, Oregon

What Is Magick?

Religion is a daughter of Hope and
Fear, explaining to Ignorance the
nature of the Unknowable.
                              —Ambrose Bierce

*A*sk anybody what magick is and the first
answer you get will have to do with either
the superstitious mumblings of the fanatical fundamentalist or the ridiculing rhetoric of the
senseless skeptic. The skeptic fellow has got one up
on our fundamentalist friend in that he can still
control some of the activity in his brain. There is
hope for this one.

1

Aleister Crowley wrote such a thorough essay on this subject that I find myself incapable of adding anything which does not echo his definition. Read the introduction of his opus *Magick in Theory and Practice.*

Aleister Crowley defines magick as **"the Science and Art of causing Change to occur in conformity with Will."**

Ambrose Bierce defines magic as "An art of converting superstition into coin."

Notice the difference in the spelling.

To distinguish illusionary magic from real magick, Crowley chose to use the Elizabethan variation of the word, in order to distinguish it from "slight of hand magic" by adding the K at the end. This changes the numerical value of the word and should be studied.

One must keep in mind that magick demands repetitious study. It is foolish to assume you have understood something unless you have read it several times and have been able to achieve the same results every time you use it. Do your experiments as though you were a scientist in a laboratory. *Keep a diary!*

Magick is the method by which all things (be it conscious or not) exist and live their lives. Magick will allow you to recognize who and what you are so that you may realize your full potential; however, it will not transform you into something which you are incapable of being.

So much beauty and mystery is found in the surviving literature of those who practiced the Craft that many artists are instinctively drawn to magick by verse and song. Ceremonial magick is the physical expression of the great struggle of evolution put into mystical dance; it is the essence of what we have been, what we are now, and the attempt to assist Nature, Our Great Mother, in what we are to become by self-discovery and by assisting in our further development.

In order to understand how magick works, a few things must be said about the mind. Not only does the brain store memory, it is also capable of behaving as a receiver. It registers memory and then executes the appropriate response. Thought and information are maintained within our cells. The DNA of which we are composed carries within it not only genetic information, but specific experiences, thoughts, and patterns of personality from our parents. This is often what a person experiences in "past life" episodes.

Genetic information is picked up by the brain once energy (memory) is released by the cells of which we are composed. The brain does all this in its effort to answer those haunting questions: Who am I? Where do I come from? Where am I going?

Each cell is a separate, living, conscious, life form, just as we are. The problem is that we are not, as a rule, consciously capable of releasing the data within the cell.

For the most part we are created and shaped according to other peoples' fancies. It starts very early in childhood when our parents (being ignorant of their own wills) impose certain things on us that may not have anything to do with our True Selves. As a result people live their lives to please those around them instead of recognizing who they truly are. The longer we are forced to do this, and the deeper we hide ourselves, the harder it is for us to find who we truly are.

There are three series of manuscripts which combined have become the source of knowledge for the modern-day magician. They are:

- The books of Solomon *(The Key of Solomon the King* and *The Lesser Key of Solomon)*

- The writings of John Dee

- *The Book of the Sacred Magic of Abramelin the Mage*

The books of Solomon are believed to have been written between 100 and 400 AD. They are based on the myths found in the Old Testament, the Talmud, and the Koran revolving around Solomon the King, the author of Proverbs, Ecclesiastes, the Song of Songs, and Wisdom.

With the assistance of demons subdued by a ring given to him by the angel Raphael, Solomon built a temple dedicated to the evocation, prosecution, classification, and identification of malignant spirits. This manuscript included information as to what names were used to call them and constrain them, as well as an elaborate hierarchy based on their power and abilities. He forced demon after demon to concede their name, power, and the name of the angel who could be called to control them. This work is seen as the greatest contribution to ceremonial magick by those who practice it, as it is a very complete genealogical tree; a source for Persian, Greek, Jewish, and Christian mythology.

The second series is a compilation of elusive writings received during several crystal gazing sessions by two Elizabethan magicians named John Dee and Edward Kelley, from 1582 to 1587. Dr. Dee anticipated that one could better communicate with the angels of God if they could speak in their tongue. He hired Edward Kelley, a medium, to communicate with various angels, who would eventually divulge their language: **Enochian.** This strange speech was believed to be the language which Adam used to communicate with the angels before the Great Fall.

With the help of several angels, Dee and Kelley were able to compose five elemental tablets describing a hierarchy of specialized angels who could be summoned to the service of the magician.

The names written on these tablets were thought to be so powerful that they were given to Kelley in reverse, for it was believed that the angels could be accidentally invoked by concentrating on the strange characters which composed their names. Even today experienced magicians heed this warning, and dabblers are discouraged from the use of Enochian magick for their own safety.

The third manuscript comprises *The Book of the Sacred Magic of Abramelin the Mage.*

The original work was written by Abraham the Jew and presented to his son Lamech in 1458. It is very likely that Abramelin was to Abraham what Aiwass was to Crowley—a discarnate being who communicated specific principles to its human counterpart.

This manuscript was found at the Bibliotheque de l'Arsenal in Paris and was translated from its Hebrew form to French during the 17th or 18th century. Later, MacGregor Mathers translated the French copy into English.

Perhaps the most significant contribution made by this book is that, while it is emphasized that one become familiar with qabalistic principles, the author strongly recommends that the student use and consecrate his own language by using it in these rites. It is universal in its message, which states that any student, whether Jewish, Christian, or Pagan, command and exercise authority over the demons mentioned in the book by using the Names of Power associated with his faith.

The manuscript was divided into three books. The first book contains personal advice from Abraham to his son and an account of how he came by this knowledge. The second book is perhaps the most important from a seeker's point of view; it is a complete treatise on the methods used to access magical powers. The third book deals with the implementation and management of this capacity.

Like the book of Solomon and the Enochian works of Dee and Kelley, the book of Abramelin the Mage is outdated in that it subscribes to the doctrine that one must isolate himself from society in order to accomplish the Great Work. In spite of this apparent Old Aeon dogma, the importance of this book cannot be underestimated, for it was through the practices laid out in this manuscript that Aleister Crowley achieved Knowledge and Conversation with his Holy Guardian Angel.

There appears to be a tradition of burning one's works at the time of one's death. Both Solomon and Dee are rumored to have burned their memoirs. If this is in fact true, then one would think that what we possess of these great men and women is very little in comparison with what must have perished by fire. For one reason or another, on April 10, 1586, Dee burned all of his works. However, according to the chronicles left behind, on April 30, while strolling through a garden in the castle of Trebona, Dee found the books he had deliberately burned on the 10th.

Among other things, magick is an ancient form of what is currently referred to as psychoanalysis. It is often used as a means to free the real Self from the self which has been created by others. The magician takes a hidden and sometimes hideous part of consciousness (as in Goetic work, the evocation of demons) and externalizes it to better deal with it. Through magick we make the necessary adjustments to achieve a healthier and better balanced individual.

Magick is the way by which one can obtain consciousness of the activity and infinite wisdom within us all. And by doing so, magick helps us to see ourselves as we truly are so that we may plot our course accordingly.

As soon as you recognize the deity within, you will find that you have been in control the whole time but have not responded well due to your lack of understanding. It is like driving with a blindfold.

The strength of your will is measured by your ability to respond (rather than react) to your environment. When you embrace life, and when you can willingly experience it as it is, then you will have embraced with Our Lady of the Stars.

The Qabalah

Nothing is a secret key of this law.
Sixty-one the Jews call it; I call it eight,
eighty, four hundred & eighteen.
                              —Liber AL I.46

*I*t is hard to pinpoint the exact date of the creation or the origin of the qabalah; however, the earliest qabalistic manuscript in our custody is called the *Sepher Yetzirah*, otherwise known as the *Book of Formation*. This text is thought to have been compiled from much older manuscripts around 120 AD, by a man called Rabbi Akiba.

The most crucial book to the study of the qabalah is called the *Zohar*. While this manuscript was not penned until the late 13th century by Moses de Leon, it is the most significant treatise connecting Gnosticism with other ancient mystical systems.

The qabalah is unique to Hebraic thought. Traditionally, it is thought that the teachings were brought out of Egypt by the Israelites. During the Babylonian captivity the Israelites borrowed from the Chaldeans the use of the "flame alphabet" and the use of numerology we call "gematria."

It is worth mentioning here that the Biblical hero named "Moses" was raised as an Egyptian and was taught the mysteries of that race of people. Later he was versed in Hebrew mysticism by his own clan. Perhaps it was the combination of both of those systems which enabled him to become such a powerful figure in history.

According to ancient Hebraic tradition, the qabalah was first disclosed to the angels by God Himself. When man was taken out of Eden, God allowed the archangel Ratziel (the archangel of wisdom) to divulge its secrets to the human race as a means for them to find their way back to the Paradise they had lost.

Again, the qabalah is unique to Hebraic thought, and as you will notice, it uses a lot of Hebraic language and symbolism. However, we will not limit its use by dwelling too much on the dogmatic aspects of this ancient system.

The reason for ignoring dogma is quite simple; the Hebraic faith has used this model for quite some time, and the impressions from the thousands who have meditated on the symbols are there for us to access. During the centuries, especially during the medieval era, the qabalah was widely dispersed throughout Europe. Magicians and their apprentices of every school of thought have meditated upon its symbols, adding to it the archetypes unique to their systems. For this reason the qabalah is richer in metaphysical wisdom than ever.

The qabalistic icon we call the "Tree of Life" is frequently mentioned in the Old Testament. This tree contains ten fruits called the "Sephiroth" (emanations). These have been referred to as "the ten faces of God"; and since humans were created in the image of God, the Tree of Life is a metaphor for the body of man (see illustration on page 11).

These ten emanations are symbols that illustrate the vigor and power of the creative energy inherent in the first sphere, Kether, the Crown, moving as swiftly as a lightning flash, changing with every step through ten varying phases which come to completion at the tenth sphere of Malkuth, the Kingdom. It attempts to describe the creation of the Universe, and those who have studied science will have to admit that, as primitive as it may be, it serves as a basic symbol illustrating the "big bang" theory. These spheres are connected by 22 Paths. The Paths correspond to the Tarot's Major Arcana.

In a way, the Sephiroth attempt to describe certain traits of the Most High, or the Universe ... or both. They are here listed in order from the Beginning to the End:

1. **Kether,** Crown. The whole of Creation concentrated to a minuscule point

2. **Chokmah,** Wisdom

3. **Binah,** Understanding

4. **Chesed,** Mercy

5. **Geburah,** Power

6. **Tiphareth,** Beauty

7. **Netzach,** Victory

8. **Hod,** Splendor

9. **Yesod,** Foundation

10. **Malkuth,** Kingdom

The manifestation of the Universe is illustrated by the union of Kether, Chokmah, and Binah. This merger composes the "Supernal Triad," which is referred to as "God" (Elohim) in Genesis. The remaining seven Sephiroth represent the seven days of creation also spoken about in the legend of Genesis.

The Hebrew qabalah is liberally used throughout four of the five books attributed to Moses. The reason for its very limited use in Deuteronomy is unknown.

In magick the qabalah is used as a filing system where one can synthesize any phenomenon whatsoever, no matter how abstract, and break it down into terms which can be understood by the logical mind.

Another use for this system is that it enables us to tap into the forces and currents symbolized by the particular symbol we are working with. The magician looks up the correspondences to the Sephiroth and uses the information to invoke that particular current.

This use of qabalistic correspondences is a science which has been created on the premise that there is an existing inherent relationship between planets, metals, stones, animals, flora, colors, and aroma. The implements, tools, incense, and colors that the magician uses will thus be in some way connected with the Sephiroth which best conveys his or her Will. This will be explained in more detail later.

Since the alchemists perceived illness to be caused by a planetary imbalance, this system was also used widely by alchemists to find cures for the ill. The cures were created by balancing the energies from the planet that was responsible for the disease and using the herbs and potions attributed to the Sephirah representing the opposite planet on the Tree of Life, thus, finding balance.

While the qabalah is not essential to magick, it will help you to understand associated phenomena. It is a system of correspondences that enables us to encounter the macrocosm by close scrutiny of the microcosm: "As above, so below."

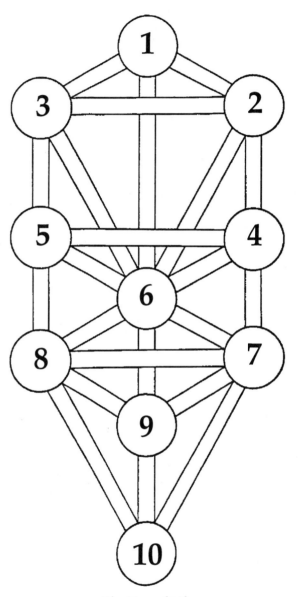

The Tree of Life

Gematria

Divide, add, multiply, and understand.

—Liber AL I:25

*A*lthough gematria is congruent to the qabalah, I think it should be treated as a separate issue in order to better explain the practical aspects of this wonderful system.

The theory here is that any words that enumerate to the same value have something in common. Perfect examples of this are found all throughout the Holy Scriptures in statements such as "God is

Love" or "Love is Unity." The idea behind gematria is that words can be replaced with other words of the same numerical value, thus revealing certain hidden mysteries. One is not limited to the Hebrew language; this method of qabalistic analysis can be used on just about any holy book so long as one becomes familiar with the numerical value of the language it was written in.

The ancient Jews did not use numerical symbols. Instead they attributed numerical values to their already existing "sacred alphabet." Unfortunately this system is perceived by the vulgar only as another form of numerology, thereby disregarding the complexity, beauty, and brilliance of such profound thought.

The importance of the use of gematria cannot be overstressed, especially when attempting to unravel the mysteries of the Bible. The authority of Biblical interpreters who are not familiar with qabalistic principles and claim to have fully disclosed its teachings is questionable. Here is why:

- The Pentateuch was written in Hebrew, and most of the works show the use of the qabalah.

- The English interpretation (or any other but Hebrew for that matter) lacks the numerical symbolism of the words written therein. They are lost in the translation; therefore, the inner meaning of the Scriptures cannot be understood by anyone not possessing knowledge of the system.

One would make a great error in assuming that this form of analysis does not apply to the New Testament because it was written in Greek. There is also Greek gematria, and there is evidence that it was used in the New Testament also. Here's an example from the book of Revelation; it deals with the Four Horseman of the Apocalypse. "And I saw, and behold a white horse: and he that sat on him had a bow; and a crown was given unto him: and he went forth conquering, and to conquer" (Rev. 6:2).

This particular passage deals with three crucial clues: the color white, the bow, and the crown. The color white is the color of Light, representing purity and cleanliness. The bow is a symbol of "Sagittarius the Archer," or one whose arrows are pointed at spiritual targets. It represents the longing to attain to spiritual heights. "Crown" is *Kether* in Hebrew, the first, white Sephiroth on the Tree of Life.

So, as you can see, the Scriptures take on a completely different meaning when you understand the methods in which they were written.

It is not necessary to become fluent in Hebrew, Latin, or Greek, but it wouldn't hurt to be at least familiar with the qabalistic correspondences of the letters of these ancient languages.

If you look at the Tree of Life, you will notice that each Sephirah has a Hebraic name and each Path has a Hebrew letter assigned to it. To reap the fruit from this Tree you will have to labor to master its language. There are only a few correspondences to commit to memory, and I have listed them for you elsewhere in this book (pages 174–7) to facilitate reference.

To conserve space, I have only demonstrated here a single form of analysis, but there are many others you will soon develop as you use this system.

The Great Work

Without faith, Science leads to doubt; without Science, faith leads to superstition. Uniting them brings certainty, but in so doing they must never be confused with each other. The object of faith is hypothesis, and this becomes certitude when the hypothesis is necessitated by evidence or by the demonstration of science. The acknowledgment of this link-up between the two basic elements of man's life results in tranquility of mind and peace of heart.

—Eliphas Levi

*T*he Great Work consists of the sublime unity of Man and Spirit. In the mysteries, Man is symbolized by the pentagram and the Spirit of God is symbolized by the hexagram.

The union of Man and Spirit could be symbolized by the 11-pointed star (5 + 6 = 11). Eleven is therefore the number of magick. This indicates that the aim of magick is union with God. In the Order of the Silver Star, the grade that symbolizes this union is called 5=6 (Man embodies God), symbolizing that the marriage has been accomplished.

There is a Word that symbolizes this Union: ABRAHADABRA. It has 11 letters and it contains five vowels, each of which is an A (the pentalpha, or pentagram, of five points). It also contains six consonants (the hexagram, six points). By the holy art of gematria this word enumerates to 418. Careful study of this number will reveal several mysteries.

The Great Work means different things to different people, but on one level it is the method by which we become one with God. The methods by which we attain these heights are to be found in the Middle Pillar on the Tree of Life.

Malkuth = Know Thyself

Yesod = Discover your True Will

Tiphareth = Knowledge and Conversation with the Holy Guardian Angel

Kether = Union with God

The Great Work is the path of return towards God. The task is not an easy one.

Self-discipline, or discipline of the mind, is the key in the beginning. Once you can quiet the mind and concentrate your thoughts on any given subject or object, the Work becomes almost second nature.

The next step is to discipline the body. Here you must learn to find specific positions in which your body can be both comfortable and rigid. This is referred to as **asana** (see illustrations, page 134).

Next, you must gain control over your breathing. As a rule, humans (with the exception of a few athletes) do not know how to breathe properly. The full potential of the lungs is not realized. This is important in the Work because oxygen is carried from the lungs into the blood stream and is then carried to the brain to vitalize brain activity. In essence, one who knows how to breathe properly has a healthy mind. Too much oxygen is as unfavorable as not enough. The practice of breath control is called **Pranayama.**

As previously stated, the brain needs a specific amount of oxygen in order to operate properly. The Hindu alchemists discovered a responsive connection between breathing patterns and the amount of energy residing in the spinal column which is called **Kundalini.**

The Kundalini is understood as a current of raw energy which dwells at the base of the spine and is capable of springing straight up the spinal column to the third eye region. When this occurs, great magically related phenomena are believed to take place. Sex is said to stimulate this coiled serpent. The other method is controlled breathing.

Breathing through the left nostril is said to stimulate a negative magnetic current called **Ida.** The properties of Ida are characteristic of **Luna,** but some believe it to be more congenial to **Venus.**

Breathing through the right nostril is understood to arouse a positive magnetic current called **Pingala.** The elements of Pingala are parallel to **Sol,** although some would argue that it is more closely related to **Mars.**

When one alternates breathing through each nostril, these subtle energies ignite the coiled snake and entice it to rise up a hollow tube that runs the length of the spine; this is called **Sushumna.**

Therefore, the purpose of Pranayama or breath control is to awaken the latent energies inhabiting our bodies. For more on Pranayama, see Practical Exercises (page 159).

The Holy Guardian Angel vs. God

Be strong, o man! lust, enjoy all things
of sense and rapture: fear not that any
God shall deny thee for this.

—Liber AL II.22

*T*wo people can look at a pencil and agree
that it is a pencil because the senses have
sent their brains similar information. However, since two objects cannot occupy the same space
at the same time, our perceptions will vary because
our positions relative to the pencil will differ.

This illustrates the great fall of conventional
religion. Every sect has a perspective of God that

differs from other sects, and they will not allow any deviance from their perspective. They fail to realize that the experience of the knowledge of God is different to every one depending on where that person is in relation to the rest of the Universe.

"God," as a word, attempts to describe an entity that admittedly cannot be described, yet those who use this word while preaching claim they know what "God" wants you to do. If "God" wants to tell you something, God will tell *you* personally.

According to the Scriptures, God wanted people to think independently, and for this reason more and more qabalists subscribe to the idea that it was God who disguised Himself as a Serpent to "tempt" Adam and Eve.

A gnostic (one who *knows* God, as opposed to one who has *faith* in the existence of God) must strive to develop a personal relationship with God, without the middle man. All that is necessary to accomplish this is within our hearts; this is the mystery of the Christ. Conventional religious cults do not want you to know this. They want you to feel like you need them; this way they can continue selling real estate in heaven. Cults need to exercise control over their members; they are not in the least bit interested in their devotees developing a personal relationship with God.

Everyone should strive to create a personal religion according to individual Will and evolutionary development. It is a good idea to study all religions in order to understand the inner mysteries hidden therein. Only by this knowledge can you come to the understanding necessary to create your own myth. Religion has a lot to offer, and you can learn much about the culture and lives of the people who follow the religion that you are researching.

Remember that, since Truth is beyond speech, it cannot be communicated. Therefore, in order to avoid folly when reading any holy book, you must not take the literal meaning as the Truth or you will be in danger of falling into the same trap as the fundamentalist. Furthermore, don't trust anyone who claims to know the Truth. Truth is protected from the vulgar because it is written in a language that only the initiated will understand. Become worthy of the Truth and it will find you. The experience of "God" differs because God manifests Itself to the individual according to individual circumstances, race, culture, education, and previous experience.

Because the Thelemic magician understands this basic principle of philosophy, Thelema uses the term **Holy Guardian Angel** when referring to a personal "God." The Magician knows that the image in which God has manifested Itself to the individual is only one in an infinity at Its disposal.

Conventional philosophies go to great lengths to make one believe that their God is the only one. They boast about Its Omnipotence and Omnipresence, yet they fail to recognize that very same God as manifested in other cultures. In essence, they blaspheme the same God that they claim to serve.

The Holy Guardian Angel is your God. It will not make you drop to your knees or expect you to do the will of others. It will walk with you, be there in times of need to comfort you, and in times of great opposition It will be the blood that boils within you. It will laugh with you in times of great happiness and strengthen you in times of great sorrow.

The image that your angel has given you is uniquely yours. Remember to show others the benefit of knowing their own God, as the sages of time tell us, **"In true religion there is no sect. Therefore take heed that thou blaspheme not the name by which another knoweth his God for if thou doest this thing in Jupiter, thou wilt blaspheme YHVH; and in Osiris YEHESHUAH.**

'Ask of God and ye shall have,
Seek, and ye shall find.
Knock, and it shall be opened unto you!' "

PERCEPTION IS NINE TENTHS OF THE LAW.

True Will
vs. Destiny

Nothing resists the will of man, when
he knows the truth, and wills the good.
—Eliphas Levi

*T*he best way to explain the difference
between True Will and destiny is to illustrate the way in which they affect our lives.
The difference between them will reveal one of the
many differences between Christianity and gnosis.

True Will is congruent with what most people
refer to as destiny, but there is one difference that
goes far beyond the literary sense of both words.

Destiny implies a predetermined course that you must travel and over the outcome of which you have no control. Your destiny is yours, like it or not. You are a pawn in a game called "life." You pray diligently to your God that you may be a worthy candidate for heaven, knowing all along (according to Christian thought) that God has already decided the outcome. To make matters worse, God won't even say what it is!

Destiny is also a convenient tool for blaming your problems on life, on the universe, and even on the God to which you pray. It is people's way of getting even with God for being so silent.

True Will, on the other hand, implies *choice and purpose.* It is for those few who choose a more responsible approach in their role as co-creator of the Universe. These people do not plead nor beg for their God's acceptance; **they are what their God has made them and for that they make no apologies.**

It could be said that True Will is Destiny transmuted into a form which allows you an active roll in your existence.

Once you find your True Will, you begin to see the deity that dwells within you. It then becomes unavoidable that you also recognize the deity dwelling in all other Stars. And there is a great consequence of this power: that which you wish upon some other, you also invoke upon yourself. Every word, deed, and thought must be pure in nature, so that it will lead you to the unity of all things.

Transmuting
Destiny
into True Will

"The will of the just man is the Will of
God himself, and the law of Nature."
—Eliphas Levi

*A*s a Magician, your first task is to find your
destiny by studying the chain of events
that have led you to your present physical,
emotional, spiritual, and mental states. By review-
ing specific events, and spending considerable time
meditating on them, you will eventually come to an
understanding of yourself and where you are going.
Thus you will discover your destiny. **Know thyself**
has always been the foundation of our Work.

Write your life story and review it often. It will have to be rewritten many times. This simple exercise will illustrate that every conclusion we come up with at any given time is an illusion which is very convenient, but tentative at best.

The next step is to magically turn the tables around and get control of a seemingly uncontrollable force. Here the magician plays an unsurpassable game of "if you can't beat 'em, join 'em." He attaches himself to his destiny through an act of Love.

Once this has been successfully accomplished, the magician experiences a series of phenomena that change destiny into True Will. You come to the realization that there is no other path you would rather travel. Because you are one with it, you can now play an active part in fulfilling it. You are no longer a prisoner to that which used to lead you by the nose. Instead, you are an agent in your own creation. Because you are now going with the current of the universe, you have the inertia of the universe behind you. Destiny has been transmuted into True Will.

The Philosophy
of True Will

To find the central clue to our moral
being which unites us to the universal
order, that indeed is the highest human
attainment. For a long time people
have seldom been capable of it.

—Confucius

*A*s I have mentioned previously, doing your
True Will means following the course
which the universe has chosen for you and
staying on it. Staying on course is very easy once
you know what your Will is, but perhaps the hard-
est part of all is not allowing others to interfere and
simultaneously being vigilant not to interfere with
the Will of others.

"Every man and every woman is a star." This is to say that everyone has a personal course which is unique to the individual. No matter how insignificant it may seem to you, your Will plays an important role within the divine plan. Just as the stars in the heavens spend millenniums traveling through the cosmos in perfect harmony, if one should veer off of its course and collide with another the whole universe would be affected. It is equally chaotic if we interfere with another. Try to imagine a world where everyone followed his or her Will and encouraged fellow human beings to do the same!

Let's study the opening phrase of this book; it's an important factor in this philosophy. No, more than that, it is our Law. **"Do what thou wilt shall be the whole of the Law."** I have often greeted people with this sentence, and it has always been received cheerfully by everyone except those who know that their intentions, motivations, and desires are anything but pure. Let me remind you that this does not imply "do what you want," because most of the things we desire only gratify the ego and have no real value. Will may be related to, may be the same as, or may be the complete opposite of want.

The word "thou" is taken from the Hebrew *ateh,* which was used by the ancients when addressing God. This sentence gives you as a human being the right to carry out your Will, presuming that you have united with it and are truly following the course chosen for you by your God. It is a lawful and noble task. One must constantly keep in mind the rules set forth above, and never interfere with the life of another *in any way, shape, or form.* I am referring to the divine Will, which is yours when you have unselfishly given yourself to it and to the service of mankind. As you have noticed, **"Love is the law, love under will"** is the second half of the formula.

This philosophy has no beginning and no end. **"Do what thou wilt"** leads you to do as you love, but keeps it in check with your Will. We all do what we want, but what we want should be what we, in good conscience, Will. Of course, this has been simplified in order to illustrate some of its many implications.

This concept implies that Love and Will are congruent, and that the only way to unite with Will is through love. Doing your Will is an act of love for humanity, the universe, and your God.

Who but a person in love would sacrifice so much of his or her life to aid and participate in the divine plan? Our goal is to evolve, to be "more than human"; but before we can start, we must possess a superhuman ability to love.

Ordeals

The more obstacles the will sur-
mounts, the stronger it is. It is for this
reason that Christ glorified poverty
and sorrow.

—Eliphas Levi

*W*hen you stray from your course you
can expect to encounter opposition.
This is not to say that if you have
discovered your True Will you will not suffer. After
all, movement creates friction. Those of us who are
going to live our lives on our own terms will have to
be willing to take a few punches from time to time.

All you have to do is read about the ailments associated with inactivity in order to agree that it is better to experience the ordeals that life offers us than to restrict movement and growth. It doesn't take much imagination to speculate about the spiritual disorders caused by inertia.

The universe has many lessons to teach, and some come in the form of ordeals. Sometimes knowing "what is to be" is saddening enough, just as I'm sure it must have been for both Jesus and Judas in the Christian legend.

Balance is the basis of the Work of the macrocosm; as the microcosm we must assist by keeping harmony within ourselves. We do this by following and staying on our Paths. When we stray, the scale tips and the universe has to compensate. This compensation, more often that not, manifests itself in an unpleasant form.

Karma and the ordeals I am referring to here are the same thing. When you have created an imbalance, the universe will present you with the situation best suited to correct this imbalance as quickly and effectively as possible.

No matter how painful the ordeal may be, it must be treated as an adventure. Keep in mind that up until this point every ordeal's purpose has been to prepare you for the kind of life you are now living. See where current circumstances are leading you, and how they are changing your life, and use this information to find out where you are going. It is an honor to know that you have been worthy of instruction. Remember that you placed yourself where you are now. Remember the ancient dictum: "I will interpret every phenomenon as a particular dealing of God with my Soul."

Knowledge

The decisive question for man is: Is he related to the infinite or not? That is the telling question of his life. Only if we know that the thing which truly matters is the infinite can we avoid fixing our interests upon futilities and upon all kinds of goals which are not of real importance.

—Carl Jung

Knowledge as applied to magick is very different from conventional knowledge. In a rapidly expanding scientific age where computers are as common as automobiles, the word "knowledge" has come to mean "having information." This is very different when it comes to the magical art.

Today's "magician" behaves as though someone has unscrewed the top of his or her head and vomited Regardie's *Golden Dawn* and Crowley's *Magick in Theory and Practice* into it. Rather than using the superb instruction offered by such books in order to gain mastery over ritual, the student repeats what is read but is unable to contribute anything new. Knowledge, to a real magician, is experience.

I have said elsewhere that one cannot "know" what an apple tastes like despite another's efforts to describe it. The advantage of having knowledge of a particular subject is that the response from a particular action is somewhat predictable.

A dabbler may have a lot of information about magick and talk a great deal about make-believe successes, but only the magician will have enough knowledge to determine the outcome of any specific ritual. Like children, we learn by doing.

Knowledge outlasts time, but information is constantly being replaced by updated information; it has no endurance. Strive therefore, to experience all things rather than just collect information. Gathering information is for those who, because of their fear of death, experience life through the eyes of brave men.

Courage

Courage means being afraid and sad-
dling up anyway.

—John Wayne

*P*erhaps the biggest pitfall for magicians is
fear. Fear manifests itself as a lack of
knowledge. Anything not understood can
create a feeling of fear towards a subject, idea, or
object. This is because in each case, the mind tries
to anticipate the future from the experience of the
subject by calling up all information related to the
experience. If there is insufficient information, a

fear of the unknown manifests. This fear can interfere with your efforts by making you feel incompetent, thus persuading you to abandon the Work.

The most dangerous fear is created by things which are *half understood*. When your mind calls up the data associated with the experience it comes up with a few bits and pieces of "self manufactured" preconceptions created by what little and incomplete information you may retain in consciousness.

While the following illustration may be somewhat crude, it serves by making a point: Take the child who touches the stove and is burned. If he or she is not instructed that ovens aren't always hot, or in the proper behavior around hot appliances, it then becomes possible that the child, upon growing up, will have some distorted image of ovens the rest of his or her life. The fear created by this process will prevent the person from discovering a sane method by which to utilize these appliances.

Fear is a built-in safety device that keeps us from repeating mistakes. But when it dominates what we think and do based on misconception, it has become our master. This is why it is so important to finish the Work you have started. If you leave anything half-finished, it will only be half-understood, leaving the phantasm in your mind with the grim chore of finishing it for you ... in any way it can.

Love

Love is a God; Strong, free, un-
abounded, and as some define Fears
nothing, pitieth none

—Milton

*L*ove is one of the trickiest things to talk about because the word has had so much untruth pumped into it.

The underlying essence of real Love is uncon-
ditional. *You cannot Love one thing and not love another.* The delusion that you can separate yourself from any other thing is created by the ego, which uses lust of result, bigotry, or a false pride as

its weapons. This kind of love usually hurts or wounds, and when we feel the prick of its thorn many of us learn to shut ourselves off to authentic Love. Our hearts harden like tempered steel. Every time we confuse love with Love we become a little more calloused and resistant. This may happen to such an extreme that when Love comes our way it is confused with the lesser love and is not allowed to find its true place within our hearts. A very perceptive man once said that the only kind of falling which is not failing is falling in Love.

The kind of Love referred to in conjunction with magick is, for the most part, unknown to most people. When one's life is being lived to its fullest potential, and all the little ordeals which come our way when we stray from our path have disappeared, that's when we are likely to experience Love.

It manifests itself as "gold." Everything you look at suddenly has a golden aura around it. There is a feeling of excitement and rediscovery. The things you took for granted have suddenly changed. They must be re-experienced under this new Light. You are likely to experience new-found trust and hope in people because you are able to recognize the deity within them. Everything is possible now. You have become as a child.

Love is Unity. Meditation is impossible without it. Every time that we attempt to fully experience another object we must unite with it. Without the ability to Love we cannot do this. When dealing with other people this could, and usually does, manifest in sex.

Sex can be the highest sacrament, but it must be brought from a *nephesh* (animal consciousness) level to a level of *nashama* (highest aspirations of the soul). This is only possible if the act is being motivated by the unifying factor within Love.

Being able to unite with object and subject is only a small step into the countless possibilities of the experiences dealing with Love. When you have mastered Love you will have completely united with it, so that it burns and communicates to others through you. You will then have harnessed that mysterious energy which turns lead into gold.

In those scarce times when two people feel pure, unadulterated Love for each other, an astral bond is created. Often psychic phenomena may be experienced as an inner rapport is created between individuals. "Love is the law, love under will": one of the many mysteries of this law is to love all creation. By so doing the magician will develop an astral connection with the whole of the cosmos.

All in all, Love is a rare commodity in this world. It doesn't come often. When it does you should be prepared to recognize it. If you are fortunate enough to find someone to love, consider what a privilege it is that this person has found you worthy of sharing their universe. Respect them, recognize their right to be themselves, to be free-thinking individuals, and then embrace them as loosely as you can.

Silence

> Let us be silent, that we may hear the whispers of the gods.
>
> —Emerson

Of the four magical powers, Silence is perhaps one of the most important. It can prevent some very painful situations in your life.

The previous aeon has left a very dangerous kind of poison in the "group mind" of Western civilization. You have only to look at history to realize that everything of value which the holy books had to offer was altered by those in authority in order to make slaves of the simple man.

The "Church" has been in power so long, and the Scriptures inaccurate for so many generations, that even its leaders are in the dark as to the true meaning of their manual.

Conventional religions preach that all one must do is to believe. You are not to question the Scriptures. This was done to prevent free thinking, and as a result the masses have become gullible, lazy, and easily controlled by those in power. To find truth in anything one must have a thirst for knowledge; one must question all things. It takes a lot of hard work. Western religion with its dogma has created a breed of humans who do not question the motives of those in authority and are too lazy to seek truth for themselves. They believe anything their superiors tell them because their superiors appear to have done the work they have avoided.

What does this have to do with Silence?

Study the history of the Church and you will see how many innocent people have been tortured and killed simply because they would not submit their will to them. How many cultures has it completely erased by "making good Christians out of savages"? How many battles have been fought in the name of the Church where good people were lost on both sides just to satisfy the lust for power and money? It has even prosecuted its own people for questioning its motives.

By keeping your Work secret, it is charged magically and it is made sacred. When ancient Egyptian adepts inherited the name of a spirit or god they zealously kept it from the profane, for by uttering the name the forces inherent in it were summoned.

Besides consecrating your Work, Silence reduces the chances of your operations being interfered with by those who are not sympathetic to magick. Do not allow doubt to enter into your Work because you have allowed others to interfere. **Test all things and hold fast to that which is good.** Enough said about ignorance.

There are other reasons why Silence is so important to magical Work.

We all know people who talk a great deal but do nothing. It would appear that talking about it brings some people more satisfaction than actually doing it.

It requires the same amount of energy (of a different sort) to talk about something and to actually do it. You can talk away your enthusiasm in a project so that when it comes down to "grounding" it, you have none.

To explain this further we have to study how thought is filtered from the archetypal plane to the material plane.

All truly great ideas believed to be inspired by genius are in fact "sparks of the divine." One who is adept in channeling such ideas has mastered the methods by which one tunes in to that plane.

These "sparks" come from the archetypal plane. These archetypes, being abstract by nature, are beyond understanding in the intellectual sense. The "spark" must go through a process of solidification and materialization, just as a fertilized egg does before being transformed into a fetus.

The spark descends downwards to the creative plane. This is the womb where all great thoughts are conceived. There it stays for a period of time until it is transformed into a symbol.

Once the creative plane has matured this symbol, it flows down to the formative plane. When it has reached this step, and not before, is when one first realizes that there is something going on in their mind that demands attention. Although it may still be a little rough, the idea is realized. It must be shaped and prepared so that it can be brought down even further and manifested in material form on the material plane.

The problems begin as soon as you become aware of the activity going on in your mind. It is easy to gratify your sense of ego by boasting of your still unmanifested project until the continuity between the higher and lower planes is disrupted. The link becomes weak, and the concept is aborted. Silence is very important indeed in magical Work.

To further illustrate the significance of Silence I include this bit of information: research done by marriage counselors showed that couples who only thought of the carnal aspects of lovemaking had no problem talking about it with others. Those couples who respected their partners and thought of their lovemaking as special would not talk about it with their counselors. They had made their lovemaking sacred.

We show this kind of devotion with our Work. Don't kiss and tell, and do not throw your pearls before swine.

Life

Beauty and strength, leaping laughter
and delicious languor, force and fire,
are of us.

—Liber AL II.20

O pportunity: the atheist looks for it, the mystic waits for it, the magician creates it.

It's easy to waste an incarnation looking and waiting. Doing and going are the functions of a god. There are many "armchair magicians" who flatter their egos by amazing their friends; talking a great deal about magick and about how efficient they have become in a particular rite. But they forget the most important object in successful ritual: **the Magical Link.** All the power that ever was, and is, and is to come is here now. Ritual is **action.** It is used to cause **change** in conformity with Will. Part of the ritual has to involve physical movement, involvement in the particular area which you are trying to change.

For example; you might feel that you need to do a ritual to change the environmental disaster that lies ahead. You can do ritual until you are blue in the face; however, unless you protest the dumping of toxic waste into the ocean, or the spraying of pesticides on our food, or the deforestation of the Amazon, there is little chance that you will have an effect. **You are the Magical Link.** The Magical Link is the object which connects the higher forces you have stimulated with the object that you are trying to affect.

What does this have to do with life? Everything! If you assume that magick is the art of living, then properly done ritual is the key to a successful life. **Every step of your everyday life should include deliberate acts of worship.**

You are the creator of your universe; you mold it, shape it, and make it what it will eventually become. If you stand idle, chances are others will shape it for you.

Live the moment now; it is the only thing that exists. The past is no longer here, and while it may have altered your evolutionary status, it is gone. The future is not here yet, so waiting for it to happen will only make you waste the precious now.

Live every moment like it is your last. Embrace life now! Experience all that is going on around you and enjoy it as a sacrament unto the Goddess, for She is experience.

There are many people who are unhappy with their lives and don't realize they hold the key to a better life in their hands! Shakespeare once said, "All the world's a stage"; if you don't like the part you are playing, change scripts!

The successful magician is one who easily adapts to his or

her environment. It is not to be conquered! You must become one with it so that you are an active player in its fulfillment, responding to situations rather than reacting.

Death

Think not, o king, upon that lie: That
Thou Must Die: verily thou shalt not
die, but live.

Liber AL II:21

As if it wasn't enough to justify one's own existence, man has also tried to discover what lies ahead after the physical body ceases to cooperate in this thing we call "life."

The deity within us all constantly plays the game of "hide and go seek." And we, being jolly good sports, play the endless game knowing that we will probably not find It. After all, it's not the kill, but the thrill of the chase. We are all hunters.

Maybe this fascination with the afterlife comes from the subconscious knowledge that we are as gods. Maybe it is one of the necessary steps in self-discovery. A lot of maybes.

We have heard countless stories from people who have died and for one reason or another have returned. While not all remembered what it was like being "clinically dead," most who *did* remember experienced images which were very similar in nature: the vision of the "white light."

We know that light is a wave that changes color according to the speed of its vibration. We see the Tree of Life as a glyph containing ten colored Spheres (which have been called "the ten faces of God") and the 22 Paths that connect them. Look at the uppermost sphere which we know as **Kether** and let's call that **Light,** fluid, moving, etc. The whole of the universe is concentrated and focused within one minuscule dot.

Now let's look at the bottom sphere, **Malkuth, the Kingdom,** the material plane, the place where all souls experience life in human bodies. Let's call that "physical existence."

The pure Light which emanates from Kether slows down as it moves away from its nucleus, changing color and becoming more "solid" as it moves away from its source. Thus, we have the other spheres on the Tree to display the different stages of this transmutation.

The ancients have told us, "Kether is in Malkuth, and Malkuth is in Kether, but after another manner," or "As above, so below." They were trying to point out that Kether was Malkuth, Light was Darkness, Fluidness was Solid, after each had been transformed by a separation which occurred within itself, a division, much like that of a cell. Malkuth is solidified Light. **We are that Light made solid.**

The Book of the Law says: "For I am divided for love's sake, for the chance of union." The Great Work is the Path of return. The return to the source. This holy book also says: "There is no bond that can unite the divided but love." This tells us that the driving force of the journey back is Love. The journey ends when we reach that Light from whence we came: Kether, union with the Goddess. We are to accomplish this union consciously.

Death is the friend of the weary traveler who has lost his way, the initiating officer to the mysteries of immortality. It is not to be feared, but welcomed as an ally and respected as the teacher that will one day provide you with the opportunity of looking at Our Lady of the Stars face to face.

Magical Organizations

Our humanity were a poor thing were it not for the divinity which stirs within us.

—Francis Bacon

*T*he function of magical orders is to serve humanity by helping the aspirants who seek its instruction to evolve, thereby assisting the whole of humanity in the evolutionary process. This should be the sole purpose for these orders.

There are several orders from which I have greatly benefited. During the occult explosion of the late 1800s, they offered instruction which was not otherwise available.

The problem with modern magical orders is that very few have kept up with the evolutionary process that their candidates have been able to access. Most of the information given in the Golden Dawn offshoots has been published by several authors over the last 50 years. Most of those who aspire to those orders have already been exposed to the material.

It is absurd to require an aspirant to quit all training simply because he or she joined with a group that, for the sake of formality, refuses to update its curriculum. It is an insult.

The aspirant is forced to take horrible oaths to keep published material secret. This will be the pitfall and eventual demise of magical orders. It would appear that most magical orders have fallen into a rut called "tradition." This inflexibility and unwillingness to evolve runs contrary to the grain of the Great Work.

From their actions, one would think that some of these orders serve the higher ups who run them instead of the aspirants who need them. We will see what fruits these orders yield in the future. Only time will tell.

The orders that are the most interested in the development of the individual are the ones that encourage individuality. Although they are ever vigilant to ensure the safety of the traveler while on the Path, they will never stifle creativity, and they are flexible enough to accommodate any seeker. The only problem with this kind of order is that it usually lacks academic structure.

In my opinion, the New Aeon magician has four orders worth mentioning at this time: an inner order known as the A∴A∴ and three outer orders which are in service to the inner known as the Ordo Templi Orientis, the Temple of Thelema, and the Fraternitas LVX Occulta. The last two groups claim lineage to the original Golden Dawn and have upgraded their curriculum to better express the current of the New Aeon.

The phenomena behind such a consolidation is quite intriguing considering that the predecessors of the Golden

Dawn would not have had much to do with Crowley *or* his system of magick.

Necessity is the forerunner of evolution. This consolidation indicates three very significant factors in today's occult community. The first is that, unlike their predecessors, the "new" Golden Dawn groups have tried Crowley's methods and have found them to be viable, sound, and practical.

The second is that most Golden Dawn fraternities have acknowledged the coming of the "new age," which Crowley delivered as Thelema. Some simply use his material and methods without disclosing the source.

The third is that, more and more, Thelemic magicians are discovering the virtues of working with other magicians; this instills upon them tolerance, discipline, and dedication to the Work.

It would be ideal if these groups succeeded in their quest to blend individuality *and* academic structure. The proof will be their success ... or failure.

THE A∴A∴

This is the order of all orders, the one of which other orders are but a shimmer of its Light. It consists of 11 grades, starting with Probationer (0=0) and ending with Ipsissimus (10=1).

There is a student period of at least three months to make sure that the aspirant is familiar with certain principles which pertain to what Crowley referred to as "scientific illuminism." During this time, the student is to study the following books and must prove that he is "thoroughly acquainted" with them and has some working knowledge of the principles described therein. The test is open book. The book list follows:

1. *The Equinox* from no. 1 to the current number

2. *Raja Yoga* by Swami Vivekananda

3. *The Shiva Sanhita* or *The Hathayoga Pradipika*

4. *Konx Om Pax*

5. *The Spiritual Guide* by Miguel Molinos

6. *Liber 777*

7. *Rituel et Dogme de la Haute Magie* par Eliphas Levi, or its translation by A.E. Waite

8. *The Goetia of the Lemegeton of Solomon the King*

9. *Collected Works*

10. *The Book of the Sacred Magic of Abramelin the Mage*

Once completed, the student takes an oath that binds him to the Work for 12 months, during which time the aspirant is referred to as "Probationer." During this time, the Probationer is instructed to become familiar with various principles, such as Pranayama and the pentagram and hexagram rituals.

Due to its appeal to most modern magicians, much lore and many untruths have been perpetuated about this holy order, some of which have discouraged many sincere and deserving students.

Perhaps the most widely spread fallacy is the assumption that membership in the order is very selective and strictly secret.

Another common misconception which is responsible for discouraging many sincere students is the tale of the mysterious oath-bound magicians of this ancient order, who spend their time secretly seeking individuals of the right mettle for the demanding, fulfilling course. We are then advised by the uninformed that we should not look for the Order, but that if we were truly ready for it, the Order would find us.

It is probable that the veil of mystery surrounding the A∴A∴ is due to the little-understood assertion that the student is to have knowledge of only two people in the Order: his instructor, and (when he has reached sufficient wisdom) the pupil he is preparing.

Each student may only move to their next grade when he or she has prepared an apprentice to take his or her place. This provides a strong, unbroken chain linking the lower with the higher.

We can turn to the application of the Probationer to dispel these myths. Please pay close attention to points 0, 4, and 8.

The Task of a Probationer

0. Let any person be received by a Neophyte, the latter being responsible to his Zelator.

1. The period of Probation shall be at least one year.

2. The aspirant to the A∴A∴ shall hear the Lection (Liber LXI) and this note of his office; IF HE WILL, shall then procure the robe of a Probationer; shall choose with deep forethought and intense solemnity a motto.

3. On reception, he shall receive the robe, sign the form provided and repeat the oath as appointed, and receive the First Volume of the Book.

4. He shall commit a chapter of Liber LXV to memory; and furthermore, he shall study the Publications of the A∴A∴ in Class B, and apply himself to such practices of Scientific Illuminism as seemeth him good.

5. Beside all this, he shall perform any tasks that the A∴A∴ may see fit to lay upon him. Let him be mindful that the word Probationer is no idle term, but that the Brothers will in many a subtle way *prove* him, when he knoweth it not.

6. When the sun shall next enter the sign under which he hath been received, his initiation may be granted unto

him. He shall keep himself free from all other engage-
ments for one whole week from that date.

7. He may at any moment withdraw from his association
   with the A∴A∴, simply notifying the Neophyte who
   introduced him.

8. He shall everywhere proclaim openly his connection
   with the A∴A∴ and speak of It and Its principles
   (even so little as he understandeth) for that mystery is
   the enemy of Truth.

   One month before the completion of his year, he
   shall deliver a copy of the Record of his year's work to
   the Neophyte introducing, and repeat to him his chosen chapter of Liber LXV.

9. He shall hold himself chaste, and reverent toward his
   body, for that the ordeal of initiation is no light one.
   This is of peculiar importance in the last two months
   of his Probation.

10. Thus and not otherwise may he attain the great reward:
    YEA, MAY HE OBTAIN THE GREAT REWARD!

Admission is not difficult, as it is stated in number 0: "Let
ANY person be received by a Neophyte …" Advancement in
this Order is not easy; it is not randomly given for the sake of
convenience or favoritism. One must *earn* one's grade; the
tasks are difficult and demanding. The lazy and insincere
aspirant seldom attains any grade beyond Neophyte.

All of those who have truly devoted their lives to the Work
are attracted to this Order the same way that a moth is drawn
to the light. If you feel this passion, use caution to avoid the
charlatans who have not yet transcended the ego. The following guidelines will help ensure that you end up with a rightful
teacher:

1. Since one must be at least a Neophyte before he or she can enroll a student, it is safe to assume that anyone claiming to be in the A.'.A.'. will have committed a chapter of Liber LXV *(Holy Books of Thelema,* Weiser, 1983) to memory (see no. 4 above). Ask the person to recite it for you.

2. Anyone claiming membership in this Order should be able to provide a clean, unbroken lineage beginning with Aleister Crowley. This information should be provided verbally, or via some documentation. If the individual is legitimate, he or she will not oppose your questioning; skepticism is an indispensable mental function required by magick.

3. Check out the names of such people by writing to the College of Thelema (C.O.T.) or the Temple of Thelema (T.O.T.); you will find their address toward the end of this book. Let them know that you were approached by someone claiming to be a member of the A.'.A.'. and you would like to make sure they have valid lineage. You may need to inform them of the lineage they are claiming. Someone there should be able to verify it. The founder of the College of Thelema retains the Jane Wolfe lineage.

It may seem like a lot of work, but believe me, it is much better to spend a lifetime looking and not finding than to waste one hour working with selfish individuals who use your pure intentions to gratify their sense of self-importance.

Magick is a *very real* thing. Anyone who can read can teach the fundamentals of knowledge and wisdom, but only a true adept can bestow upon you the power of the ages.

Everything you will ever want to know about how the A.'.A.'. functions is available in a brilliantly written work entitled *The Mystical & Magical System of the A∴A∴* by James A. Eshelman. At the present time, this highly informative text is privately printed by the College of Thelema. I would strongly recommend that anyone interested in a truthful account regarding the operations of this unique, unsurpassed system of initiation write to the address listed on the back of this book for a copy.

ORDO TEMPLI ORIENTIS (O.T.O.)

This organization was created by Karl Kellner and Theodore Reuss in the 1890s. Like the A∴A∴, the history of the O.T.O. and how Crowley became the Outer Head of the Order is filled with fables.

One of the most popular stories is that, upon publishing his *Book of Lies,* Aleister Crowley inadvertently disseminated some of the highest secrets of the Order in a treatise dealing with sex magick. Reuss, who happened to be in England at the time, held him to an oath of secrecy, and it is believed that at this time Crowley was made head of the Order in English-speaking countries.

This, so the story goes, came as quite a surprise to Crowley. The O.T.O. became the observation arena where teachers of the A∴A∴ could seek prospective students.

The actual account is much more interesting. Upset by the fact that Crowley published much of the outer order material of the Golden Dawn, MacGregor Mathers endeavored to file suit against Crowley in an attempt to block the publication of the inner order material. In order to give credibility to his testimony, Mathers stated that he was, in fact, the only head of the Rosicrucian Order.

This was taken to be quite arrogant by the Rosicrucian fraternities of the time, and their response was surprising:

Theodore Reuss was one among the many heads of fraternal organizations which bestowed various titles upon Crowley in order to add weight to *his* testimony.

During this time, it was a common practice for the O.T.O. to recognize the degrees of Masons who sought admission and to compensate them for their Masonic knowledge. The 33rd Degree in Masonry was equivalent to the 7th degree in the O.T.O., and since Crowley was a 33rd-Degree Mason, Reuss conferred upon him the 7th Degree—not the 10th, as it is rumored.

Between 1910 and 1912, Crowley worked the 7th, 8th, and 9th Degrees, and it was in 1912 that Reuss adopted *The Book of the Law* and allowed Crowley to rewrite the initiation rituals to better reflect the transition of the New Aeon. He introduced the concept of Thelema: "Do what thou wilt shall be the whole of the Law." The Ordo Templi Orientis is the first spiritual organization accepting *The Book of the Law* as their holy book.

During the early 1900s, the O.T.O. (as it existed then) experienced a loss of interest by the populace. Seeing that Aleister Crowley had become somewhat of an occult celebrity, and was admired by as many as loathed him, Reuss conferred upon him the 10th Degree in 1912. This was a maneuver to invigorate interest in the organization, and it proved to be quite successful. Crowley became Outer Head of the Order when Reuss died in 1922, many years after *The Book of Lies* had been published.

The Order now exists internationally and is recognized as a religious organization worldwide.

Membership in the Order is confidential; if you become involved, no one will inform anyone. If you want to tell someone you are a member, it is your business. All men and women of full age and in good report are entitled to the first three degrees, after which one may progress only by invitation.

The Ordo Templi Orientis has many bodies worldwide which teach and practice ritual magick. It provides its members with a free atmosphere where they can be who they truly are. The main goal of the Order is to secure the absolute freedom of its members by assisting the individual in whatever way possible to discover his or her True Identity. Since one cannot know the True Will of another, this process must be accomplished only by the individual; thus the Order can assist but not interfere with this process.

The O.T.O. is a home for many magicians of different walks of life who have accepted the Law of the New Aeon and wish to exchange ideas with those of like mind. Most of its members are influenced by Aleister Crowley, the Golden Dawn, and Wicca. It provides camaraderie and fellowship and, in places that practice the Gnostic Mass, spiritual sustenance.

TEMPLE OF THELEMA (T∴O∴T∴)

The Temple of Thelema (T∴O∴T∴) is affiliated with the College of Thelema but provides a more comprehensive outer vehicle to the A∴A∴, offering ceremonial group ritual working and much supplemental instruction. The T∴O∴T∴ is a ceremonial magical order based on the Golden Dawn temple model but conforming fully to the Thelemic dispensation of the New Aeon. It has a hierarchical structure of degrees in both outer and inner orders, based upon the model of the Tree of Life. Advancement is based on passing written examinations and completing various practices of study, ritual, and meditation. Completion of the outer order (0–4th degree) includes all of the C.O.T. course material and therefore also fulfills the A∴A∴ student requirement.

The T∴O∴T∴ meets regularly for formal ceremonial ritual workings and the development of a magical "group mind." A serious commitment of time and effort is required of each member accepted into the Order. Membership is steadily growing and temples have been established in locations throughout the world. Special provisions also exist for members without a temple in their area.

COLLEGE OF THELEMA (C.O.T.)

The College of Thelema was founded in service to the A∴A∴ in order to provide a structured approach to the preparation of students for its arduous curriculum. When Aleister Crowley began accepting Probationers into the A∴A∴, he soon found that most never made it beyond Neophyte unless they had begun with a solid grounding in occult theory and practice. To improve his success rate with new initiates, he instituted a student period to be undertaken for at least 12 months before one could become eligible for the grade of Probationer. Some of the studies undertaken by the student in Crowley's day are outlined in Appendix A of *Magick in Theory and Practice.*

Crowley's A∴A∴ student tasks were broadly defined in terms of a reading list and familiarity with various branches of learning, which still required a measure of specialized teaching to ensure adequate preparation for each individual. Responding to the need for a more standardized curriculum with a greater scope of instruction, an A∴A∴ teacher, Soror Meral, established the College of Thelema (C.O.T.) to fill this need.

The C.O.T. offers a series of courses in occult knowledge and self exploration through personalized instruction. Completion of Course I in this curriculum fulfills the A∴A∴ student requirement. Each student is assigned a teacher who works one-on-one with the student to oversee his or her progress in the course work. Much of the work can be accomplished through correspondence, although periodic personal contact is required. The College is based in Oroville, California, and offers instruction there as well as in Los Angeles and other parts of the country. Two years of prior college education are generally required; equivalences will be considered.

The College also makes available a wealth of information, much of it previously unpublished or nearly impossible to find, in its biannual journal *In The Continuum*. Back issues from Volumes I through IV (10 issues each, except vol. II with 12 issues) are available for $5 each.

THE FRATERNITY OF THE HIDDEN LIGHT

This group is more traditional in its approach to ceremonial magick, as it draws most of its wisdom from lineage to Mathers' Golden Dawn and original Rosicrucianism.

It has temples in the U.S. and Canada and, while membership is secret, it frequently performs rituals during Equinoxes or Solstices which are open to the public.

It offers the best preliminary courses in magical wisdom I have ever seen or read. The serious student who has decided to work alone without the benefit of fraternal assistance should seriously consider these courses, as they reveal much previously unpublished material.

Of course, there are many other orders. I have only commented on the ones with which I have had contact. I strongly caution the seeker to exercise caution when seeking a group to work with. Recently, it has become fashionable to conduct groups, and many have been started without proper lineage or authority of any kind. This is particularly true with Golden Dawn types. This is not to say that everyone who claims proper charter is a charlatan, but documentation should be requested before committing one's self to *any* group.

For more information regarding these organizations please refer to the contact list at end of this book.

Why Thelema?

The old gods are dead or dying and
people everywhere are searching, asking: What is the new mythology to be?
—Joseph Campbell

*A*s you read this book you may be asking
yourself: why would anyone want to
attune to a new form of thought while
there are already very powerful, well organized religions, which have had the benefit of thousands of
years of trial and error?

The answer is quite simple: there is a phenomenon that occurs in the universe every 2,000 to

5,000 years called "the Equinox of the Gods." At this time there is a change in the universal unconsciousness which dominates the evolutionary process of humans. The different shifts are represented by gods (usually Egyptian) whose virtues will demonstrate the fate of the next reign. There have been (so far as we have archaeological data) three such "shifts" in the evolution of humanity:

1. **The Aeon of Isis.** This period was matriarchal. Women were worshiped as gods for their ability to give birth, nurture, and otherwise care for their young. The tribes were ruled by queens, and the women were viewed as the strong ones. There are indications that women did the hunting and fought battles alongside of men. It was a time of great respect for nature, as people learned to love Her and live in harmony with Her.

2. **The next Aeon was ruled by Osiris.** Osiris was killed by his jealous brother Set who cut him into pieces and threw him into the Nile. His wife Isis, stricken with grief, gathered all of his body parts and used the magick of Thoth (Lord of Magick) to resurrect Osiris. It was the era of the "sacrificial gods." It marked the beginning of Judaism and Christianity. This change occurred when man realized that he had something to do with conception, primarily insemination. Suddenly women were treated as second-rate citizens, weaker, and not as intelligent as men. Man was no longer to live in harmony with Nature; man was to have dominion over Her. Mankind was to serve the male god as slaves. The last traces of this oppressive era are still with us today. We can see its influence on the environment and in places such as South Africa.

3. In 1904 another such shift occurred. The angel
Aiwass dictated the threefold *Book of the Law* and pro-
claimed that Horus, the hawk-headed God, had taken
his place on the Throne of the Gods. The Victorian
age magician Aleister Crowley was to be the conduit.
This era marks the Aeon of the Child, the word of
whose Law is **Thelema.** This Law encompasses all true
religions and is capable of great tolerance, which is
essential to protect the diversity it conveys. Here we
are dealing with the liberation of the human race from
those which have oppressed it.

Horus is the Egyptian God of war, and recently we have
seen him do his thing in Germany (at the Berlin Wall),
Yugoslavia, Poland, the Soviet Union, South Korea, and Tien-
amen Square in China. The masses cry for freedom.

The Aeon of Osiris has had a very strong influence in the
last 2,000 years. Even those who do not subscribe to its dogma
are influenced by it in one way or another. Most codes of
morality are based on its principles. This has been the case for
so long that we are presented with the opportunity to reflect
on it and see how its poison has affected the world.

It has portrayed women as troublemakers, people who
cannot keep secrets, weaker and not as intelligent as men, not
trustworthy. It has even gone so far as to explain the pain of
childbirth and menstrual bleeding as punishments from God
for having deceived man. Women in this day are still fighting
for the equality they deserve.

It has led man believe that Nature cannot go on without
him. All we have to do is watch TV or read a newspaper to find
out what a great impact we have made and how much good we
have contributed to the environment. It is inconceivable that
after millions of years of evolution there are still people who
really believe Nature is to be dominated. We are told that God
doesn't live here, and we are discouraged from showing affec-

tion or allegiance to the Earth. We can already see what this kind of thinking has done to the condition of our Mother.

The Church will not condone the use of condoms. It believes that people should just "not do it." As a result the rate of unwanted pregnancy is increasing at an alarming rate, not to mention the sexually transmitted diseases which are destroying so many peoples' lives. It is curious to see that the same people who oppose birth control also oppose abortion, sex education, and Planned Parenthood. Abortion would cease to exist if education and birth-control technology were not obstructed by religious zealots. When it comes to human sexuality, we are still in the Dark Ages.

During the "Inquisition" thousands of innocent people were tortured and killed in the name of God. Many of these people were often women (midwives) who happened to be taking business away from the growing medical profession. Things have not changed much since those days. In some states they want to jail midwives who perform their services to couples who have lost their faith in "the scientific age." In all, most decisions our political leaders make conform in some form or another with old Aeon ideas, with very little regard to common sense and intelligence, and even less consideration to the rights of the individual.

The burning and censoring of books and art still occur today. Others have controlled what we watch, see, eat, and listen to.

We have been taught that any deviance from conventional religion is "Satanic," evil, etc. On August 15, 1989, the fundamentalist movement declared on national television that the star of David, the pentagram, and even the peace sign are signs of the devil.

The hexagram, a geometric representation of God; the pentagram, a geometric representation of Man; and the peace sign, a symbol of utopian society.

It is easy to see the impact this kind of thinking has had on our global evolutionary development: brother has turned against brother for the sake of tradition, as in the case of the Catholic Priest Miguel Molinos. This devoted priest was sent to prison to serve a life sentence because he published a book in which he taught that "inward prayer" (meditation) was more effective than outward prayer. This would have made confession via a priest obsolete. The fact that at the time of his arrest he was one of the most devout members of the Church had very little influence on the power-hungry individuals who condemned him. The book he wrote is *The Spiritual Guide of Miguel Molinos.* I strongly recommend it as a guide to developing a *personal* relationship with God.

Fundamentalism spends millions of dollars printing material every year to encourage new membership while there are millions of homeless men, women, and children who could be helped by these same dollars. It is obvious that the emphasis is in membership rather than service.

For the last 2,000 years we have been told that sex is filthy. Lovemaking is to be done only for the purposes of procreation. This mentality is responsible for a great percentage of violent sexual crimes, child abuse, sexual dysfunctions, psychosis, etc. The beauty and selflessness of giving oneself to another has been turned into a hideous crime against God.

We are told not to question the Scriptures. Man has become lazy and gullible as a result. We don't question anything and believe all we are told. We are expected to refrain from our own interpretation of the Scriptures in fear that we might find truth therein. To guard against this, the Scriptures have been altered so much that no one knows the truth anymore. This has affected the way we view life in general. We do not question what our politicians do, what they spray in our food, what they put into the ground, etc. And when we do ask, we believe everything they tell us. **Thelema demands that we think for ourselves.**

A newborn child is the most innocent and pure of all things. Yet children are baptized by parents who have been forced to belieye the child is unclean because it is born through sin. This is an insult, and shows to what degree and for what "reasons" we do the things we do.

Religious zealots have created a group mind which welcomes the destruction of the planet. It is held to be a fact that before the "savior" comes back the world must first face a terrible ordeal. "Revelation" clearly marks the end of the Osirian Aeon, but it is seen through the eyes of the vulgar as the end of the world. This "group mind" has greatly affected the condition of the planet. We have a duty to return to Nature what belongs to Her. There was a time when it took years to get from one part of the country to another. We can now do it in a matter of hours; we have reduced the world to a speck of dust. With all of this technology there are still people dying of hunger all over the world. Wars are waged to keep something or to take something from someone else. When religion stands in the way of evolution or the creation of utopia, it is time for a *new* religion.

These old ideas cannot help us to further our evolutionary objective; they are full of hate and bigotry and can do nothing more than to hold the human race back. The world needs an alternative: true freedom. The world needs the freedom necessary to fulfill itself as best as it can without the interference of a twisted, demented creed that was designed specifically to control people. Nature needs to have its respect from Man. We must learn to work with Her, not against Her, and then perhaps we can stop the destruction of the planet.

With all that's been said above, it is hard to understand why anyone would bother with religion in the first place. The answer is quite simple: Man is made up of physical, mental, and spiritual matter. To deny any of these aspects a means of expressing itself would cause an involuntary imbalance in our natural make-up. Also, religion and myth are the tools the Beloved uses to create the beings which we have chosen to become; just as the potter uses the wheel and the kiln to create something which only a few moments ago existed only in the imagination of the creator.

Thelema offers the solution to the imbalance created by such an oppressive society. As humans, it is our duty to carry the vision of future generations on our shoulders by evolving. This is "the Great Work." One day the Aeon of Horus will pass, and Thelema will no longer be the Word of the Law, and a new order will rule for an Aeon. There will be other battles and principles, and it is my guess that we will be here once again to fight for them.

The following thesis is based on the code of conduct of those who accept the Law of Thelema.

DUTY
by Aleister Crowley

(A note on the chief rules of practical conduct to be observed by those who accept the Law of Thelema.)

"Do what thou wilt shall be the whole of the Law."

"There is no law beyond Do what thou wilt."

"[...] thou hast no right but to do thy will. Do that, and no other shall say nay. For pure will, unassuaged of purpose, delivered from the lust of result, is every way perfect."

"Love is the law, love under will."

"Every man and every woman is a star."

A. YOUR DUTY TO YOURSELF

1. Find yourself to be the centre of your own Universe.

   "I am the flame that burns in every heart of man, and in the core of every star."

2. Explore the Nature and Powers of your own Being.

   This includes everything which is, or can be for you; and you must accept everything exactly as it is in itself, as one of the factors which go to make up your True Self. This True Self thus ultimately includes all things soever; its discovery is Initiation (the traveling inwards) and as its Nature is to move continually, it must be understood not as static, but as dynamic, not as a Noun but as a Verb.

3. Develop in due harmony and proportion every faculty which you possess.

   "Wisdom says: be strong!"
   "But exceed! exceed!"
   "Be strong, o man! lust, enjoy all things of sense and rapture: fear not that any God shall deny thee for this."

4. Contemplate your own Nature.

   Consider every element thereof both separately and in relation to all the rest as to judge accurately the true purpose of the totality of your Being.

5. Find the formula of this purpose, or "True Will," in an expression as simple as possible. Learn to under-

stand clearly how best to manipulate the energies which you control to obtain the results most favourable to it from its relations with the part of the Universe which you do not yet control.

6. Extend the dominion of your consciousness, and its control of all forces alien to it, to the utmost.

Do this by the ever stronger and more skillful application of your faculties to the finer, clearer, fuller, and more accurate perception, the better understanding, and the more wisely ordered government, of that external Universe.

7. Never permit the thought or will of any other Being to interfere with your own.

Be constantly vigilant to resent, and on the alert to resist, with unvanquishable ardour and vehemence of passion unquenchable, every attempt of any other Being to influence you otherwise than by contributing new facts to your experience of the Universe, or by assisting you to reach a higher synthesis of Truth by the mode of passionate fusion.

8. Do not repress or restrict any true instinct of your Nature; but devote all in perfection to the sole service of your one True Will.

"Be goodly therefore"

"The word of Sin is Restriction. O man! refuse not thy wife, if she will! O lover, if thou wilt, depart! There is no bond that can unite the divided but love:

all else is a curse. Accurséd! Accurséd be it to the aeons! Hell."

"So with thy all; thou hast no right but to do thy will. Do that, and no other shall say nay. For pure will, unassuaged of purpose, delivered from the lust of result, is every way perfect."

"Ye shall gather goods and store of women and spices; ye shall wear rich jewels; ye shall exceed the nations of the earth in splendour & pride; but always in the love of me, and so shall ye come to my joy."

9. Rejoice!

"Remember all ye that existence is pure joy; that all the sorrows are but as shadows; they pass & are done; but there is that which remains."

"But ye, o my people, rise up & awake! Let the rituals be rightly performed with joy & beauty! [...] A feast for fire and a feast for water; a feast for life and a greater feast for death! A feast every day in your hearts in the joy of my rapture! A feast every night unto Nu, and the pleasure of uttermost delight! Aye! feast! rejoice! there is no dread hereafter. There is the dissolution, and eternal ecstasy in the kisses of Nu."

"Now rejoice! now come in our splendour & rapture! Come in our passionate peace, & write sweet words for the Kings!"

"Thrill with the joy of life & death! Ah! thy death shall be lovely: whoso seeth it shall be glad. Thy death shall be the seal of the promise of our agelong love. Come! lift up thine heart & rejoice!"

"Is a God to live in a dog? No! but the highest are of us. They shall rejoice, our chosen: who sorroweth is not of us. Beauty and strength, leaping laughter and delicious languor, force and fire, are of us."

B. YOUR DUTY TO OTHER INDIVIDUAL MEN AND WOMEN

1. "Love is the law, love under will."

Unite yourself passionately with every other form of consciousness, thus destroying the sense of separateness from the Whole, and creating a new base-line in the Universe from which to measure it.

2. "As brothers fight ye!"

"If he be a King, thou canst not hurt him."

To bring out saliently the differences between two is useful to both in measuring the position of each in the whole. Combat stimulates the virile or creative energy; and, like love, of which it is one form, excites the mind to an orgasm which enables it to transcend its rational dullness.

3. Abstain from all interferences with other wills.

"Beware lest any force another, King against King!"

(The love and war in the previous injunctions are of the nature of sport, where one respects, and learns from the opponent, but never interferes with him, outside the actual game.) To seek to dominate or influence another is to seek to deform or destroy him; and he is a necessary part of one's own Universe, that is, of one's self.

4. Seek, if you so will, to enlighten another when need arises.

This may be done, always with the strict respect for the attitude of the good sportsman, when he is in distress through failure to understand himself clearly, especially when he specifically demands help; for his darkness may hinder one's perception of his perfection.

(Yet also his darkness may serve as a warning, or excite one's interest.) It is also lawful when his ignorance has led him to interfere with one's will. All interference is in any case dangerous, and demands the exercise of extreme skill and good judgment, fortified by experience.

To influence another is to leave one's citadel unguarded; and the attempt commonly ends in losing one's own self-supremacy.

5. Worship all!

"Every man and every woman is a star."
"Mercy let be off: damn them who pity!"
"We have nothing with the outcast and the unfit: let them die in their misery. For they feel not. Compassion is the vice of kings: stamp down the wretched &

the weak: this is the law of the strong: this is our law and the joy of the world. Think not, o king, upon that lie: That Thou Must Die: verily thou shalt not die, but live. Now let it be understood: If the body of the King dissolve, he shall remain in pure ecstasy for ever. Nuit! Hadit! Ra-Hoor-Khuit! The Sun, Strength & Sight, Light; these are for the servants of the Star & the Snake."

Each being is, exactly as you are, the sole centre of a Universe in no wise identical with, or even assimilable to, your own. The impersonal Universe of "Nature" is only an abstraction, approximately true, of the factors which it is convenient to regard as common to all. The Universe of another is therefore necessarily unknown to, and unknowable by, you; but it induces currents of energy in yours by determining in part your reactions. Use men and women, therefore, with the absolute respect due to inviolable standards of measurement; verify your own observations by comparison with similar judgments made by them; and, studying the methods which determine their failure or success, acquire for yourself the wit and skill required to cope with your own problems.

C. YOUR DUTY TO MANKIND

1. Establish the Law of Thelema as the sole basis of conduct.

The general welfare of the race being necessary in many respects to your own, that well-being, like your own, principally a function of the intelligent and wise observance of the Law of Thelema, it is of the very first importance to you that every individual should accept frankly that Law, and strictly govern himself in full accordance therewith. You may regard the establishment of the Law of Thelema as an essential element of your True Will, since, whatever the ultimate nature of that Will, the evident condition of putting it into execution is freedom from external interference.

Governments often exhibit the most deplorable stupidity, however enlightened may be the men who compose and constitute them, or the people whose destinies they direct.

It is therefore incumbent on every man and woman to take the proper steps to cause the revisions of all existing statutes on the basis of the Law of Thelema. This Law being a Law of Liberty, the aim of the legislation must be to secure the amplest freedom for each individual in the state, eschewing the presumptuous assumption that any given positive ideal is worthy to be obtained.

"The word of Sin is Restriction."

The essence of crime is that it restricts the freedom of the individual outraged. (Thus, murder restricts his right to live; robbery, his right to enjoy the fruits of his labour; coining, his right to the guarantee of the state that he shall barter in security; etc.) It is then the common duty to prevent crime by segregating the criminal, and by the threat of reprisals; also, to teach the criminal that his acts, being analyzed, are contrary to his own True Will. (This may often be accomplished by taking from him the right which he has denied to others; as by outlawing the thief, so that he feels constant anxiety for the safety of his own possessions, removed from the ward of the State.) The rule is quite simple.

He who violated any right declares magically that it does not exist; therefore it no longer does so, for him.

Crime being a direct spiritual violation of the Law of Thelema, it should not be tolerated in the community. Those who possess the instinct should be segregated in a settlement to build up a state of their own, so to learn the necessity of themselves imposing and maintaining rules of justice. All artificial crimes should be abolished. When fantastic restrictions disappear, the greater freedom of the individual will itself teach him to avoid acts which really restrict natural rights. Thus real crime will diminish dramatically.

The administration of the Law should be simplified by training men of uprightness and discretion whose will is to fulfill this function in the community to decide all complaints by the abstract principle of the Law of Thelema, and to award judgment on the basis of the actual restriction caused by the offense. The ultimate aim is thus to reintegrate conscience, on true scientific principles, as the warden of conduct, the monitor of the people, and the guarantee of the governors.

D. YOUR DUTY TO ALL OTHER BEINGS AND THINGS

1. Apply the Law of Thelema to all problems of fitness, use, and development.

It is a violation of the Law of Thelema to abuse the natural qualities of any animal or object by diverting it from its proper function, as determined by consideration of its history and structure. Thus, to train children to perform mental operations, or to practice tasks, for which they are unfitted, is a crime against nature. Similarly, to build houses of rotten material, to adulterate food, to destroy forests, etc., etc., is to offend.

The Law of Thelema is to be applied unflinchingly to decide every question of conduct. The inherent fitness of any thing for any proposed use should be the sole criterion.

Apparent, and sometimes even real, conflict between interests will frequently arise. Such cases are to be decided by the general value of the contending parties in the scale of Nature. Thus, a tree has a right to its life; but a man being more than a tree, he may cut it down for fuel or shelter when need arises. Even so, let him remember that the Law never fails to avenge infractions: as when wanton deforestation has ruined a climate or a soil, or as when the importation of rabbits for a cheap supply of food has created a plague.

Observe that the violation of the Law of Thelema produces cumulative ills. The drain of the agricultural population to big cities, due chiefly to persuading them to abandon their natural ideals, has not only made the country less tolerable to the peasant, but debauched the town. And the error tends to increase in geometrical progression, until a remedy has become almost inconceivable and the whole structure of society is threatened with ruin.

The wise application based on observation and experience of the Law of Thelema is to work in conscious harmony with Evolution. Experiments in creation, involving variation from existing types, are lawful and necessary.

Their value is to be judged by their fertility as bearing witness to their harmony with the course of nature towards perfection.

A Better Society

Monarchy is based on the premise
that one man is wiser than one million
men. Democracy is based on the
premise that a million men are wiser
than one man. Both ideas are absurd.
—Robert Heinlein

The following is a manuscript written by
Aleister Crowley describing the nature of
the most elemental rights of every individual. It must be remembered that it was written at a
time when the English language was male dominated. Since I am not the author of this piece I am
obligated to present it in its original form.

LIBER LXXVII
OZ:

> "the law of
> the strong:
> this is our law
> and the joy
> of the world."
> —AL II.21

"Do what thou wilt shall be the whole of the law."—AL
I.40

"thou hast no right but to do thy will. Do that, and no
other shall say nay."—AL I.42–3

"Every man and every woman is a star."—AL I.3

There is no god but man.

1. Man has the right to live by his own law—
    to live in the way that he wills to do:
    to work as he will:
    to play as he will:
    to rest as he will:
    to die when and how he will.

2. Man has the right to eat what he will:
    to drink what he will:
    to dwell where he will:
    to move as he will on the face of the earth.

3. Man has the right to think what he will:
    to speak what he will:

to write what he will:
to draw, paint, carve, etch, mould, build as he will:
to dress as he will.

4. Man has the right to love as he will:—
  "take your fill and will of love as ye will,
  when, where, and with whom ye will."—AL I.51.

5. Man has the right to kill those who would thwart these rights.

  "the slaves shall serve."—AL II.58

  "Love is the law, love under will."—AL I.57

Diet

He who has health has hope, he who
has hope has everything.
—Arabian Proverb

*T*he magician can be looked upon as a bat-
tery, with the capacity to store and manipulate energy and current. Pranayama and
exercise deal with the capacity to hold these elements. Through physical movement we become
more efficient vehicles to carry with us this Life
Force. Diet deals with the energy and current. It
would be of little value to become perfect vessels if

we filled ourselves with dead matter or things of substance with little value.

In today's world we are faced with a unique problem. Science can keep us alive a lot longer than ever before, but the quality of living has gone downhill. Our environment is such that we have to depend on those methods of life extension because living in this filthy, polluted world is killing us. Even the food which we eat can harm us because of the processing which it has to go through before it gets to our tables—not to mention the pesticides which are sprayed on our fruits and vegetables, or the waxes in which they are covered in order to make them appear to be fresh.

The animals which we eat are fed antibiotics, which we absorb when eating the meat; our bodies then adjust to these accumulative levels of antibiotics until they become worthless to us in treating infection. Because the cattle rancher mixes these antibiotics indiscriminately with the cattle's food, the body of the animal ultimately becomes the perfect breeding ground for medicine-tolerant bacteria. This bacteria are then absorbed into our bodies by consuming the flesh of the animal, and because we have developed a tolerance to antibiotics we are not able to treat the ailment.

Farmers have added more and more chemicals to the soil; these are in turn absorbed by the vegetation we eat and leach into the water we drink.

Processing hurts all foods. When wheat is "refined" it loses over 20 nutrients in the process. The flour manufacturer returns four or five chemical nutrients to it and then calls it "enriched."

Wheat and bread have been subjected to about 80 chemicals in the growing and manufacturing process. Some of these chemicals stay in the finished product to be eaten by the unsuspecting consumer.

There is a substance in all living things called **Prana.** This Prana is the "life force" within them; it is responsible for the vitality of all living organisms. All vegetables, fruits, and animals have Prana; the amount is determined by the condition, biological makeup and size of the item. They get it from nutrients in the soil or food which they consume. Without it, all living things would die.

We human beings require Prana for our survival. We get it from the foods we consume, the sun we are exposed to, and the air we breathe. So it makes a lot of sense to only consume those foods which have the highest amount of Prana still in them. Prana will stay within fruits, vegetables, and meats after they have been picked or slaughtered for a time determined by the condition they were in at the point their lives were terminated.

Another dietary problem we face is that humans have much longer intestinal tracts and weaker digestive acids than most meat-eating animals. This creates two problems:

1. Human digestive acids do not break down flesh properly because they are not strong enough to do so. Therefore, most of the nutrients that are available in meat are not even absorbed by our intestines into our bodies.

2. The undigested remains of meat are sent down to our intestines where they can be absorbed into our bodies, but because the intestinal tract is so long in humans, the meat starts to rot before it can reach that stage. What we end up absorbing are the poisons in the rotten meat.

If you must eat meat chew it thoroughly, as the enzymes in your saliva are very important in the digestive and absorption processes. Saliva is believed to release Prana from foods so that it can be absorbed through the mucus membrane in the mouth.

Canned foods should be avoided. By the time the food has gone through processing and refining, it has lost 82% of its proteins, amino acids, and nutrients.

Frozen food, especially meat, is even worse. Between stock fed tetracycline, steroids, processing, and freezing there is a 92% loss. And most importantly, you cannot freeze or can Prana. The reason that frozen and canned foods "appear" fresh is because of the chemicals that are added to preserve the food. T.V. dinners, junk foods, and fast foods ought to be avoided. All chemical preservatives should be considered poisons.

Sugar, salt, and white flour are worthless. There is no food value left in these after "refining," only chemicals which are used in the process. Monosodium glutamate (M.S.G.) damages the nervous system and has been known to destroy brain cells.

Vitamin tablets should be relied upon only when the proper vitamin and/or mineral can not be extracted from food. Most vitamin tablets are chemicals, and the body has a hard time dealing with unnatural substances. They should not be taken in place of food; remember what's been said about Prana.

Vitamin supplements are useless because some mineral/vitamins prevent the absorption of others which may be included in the same pill. Take your vitamins separately at different times of the day and make sure that they are not synthetic forms of vitamins (synthetic vitamin D has been known to cause much trouble in some individuals). The best policy is to eat the right foods; **raw materials.**

Much has been said in this chapter about things which most people believe have nothing to do with magick or the Great Work, but I assure you they are mistaken. The furnace which the alchemists referred to in their books is the body! Making sure that it functions well is of great importance.

If you take the time to care for your vehicle you will see a body which is leaner, stronger, healthier, and more resistant to the stress created by a harmful environment and everyday life. Such a body is better equipped to deal with whatever you may encounter on your magical voyage, a body worthy of the Great Work.

Fasting

For many centuries fasting has been used by those seeking communion with God, and it has been used by magicians as a form of self-sacrifice in order to guarantee a successful magical result. In these times, fasting has become a method by which to rid the body of toxins.

The use of water fasts is extremely dangerous to one's body. If you are to refrain from consuming foods, juices and teas are an excellent source of nourishment while the body is being purged of its poisons. Fasting is not for everyone; one should consult a physician before radically modifying his or her diet.

Depending on your physical or psychological condition, water fasts are known to produce hallucinations, delusions, spiritual experiences, euphoria, and other symptoms associated with psychosis.

In Biblical times, fasting was very widely used to induce such states. Many men have been described in holy books as having gone into the desert without food or water and having come back more enlightened, or internally changed by some mystical experience. It is the opinion of many scholars that the lack of nourishment is what brought about these altered states of consciousness.

Other cultures, such as the American Indians, achieved the same experiences using various natural drugs (such as mushrooms or peyote), or herbal mixtures containing hallucinogenics. This is probably much safer than a water fast lasting more than ten days.

There are many methods and techniques that can be used for a successful fast that will not cause physical damage. The following method can be kept up for many months, and is relatively safe.

Again, this method is easy, safe, and can be kept up for many weeks at a time: eat only every other day. Drink as much water, juice, or tea as you wish on the fasting days, but remember that most juices contain high concentrations of acid which could cause heartburn and other gastric disturbances.

The digestive enzymes in your stomach will be diluted in accordance to how much food you consume. For this reason, on the days that you eat, refrain from eating meats or other fatty foods because these are not so easily digested and remain in your body for longer periods of time. Obviously, spicy foods should be cut down to avoid acid indigestion.

Exercise

It is only by labor that thought can be made healthy, and only by thought that labor can be made happy; and the two cannot be separated with impunity.

—John Ruskin

*P*hysical exercise helps to maintain the chemical/organic balance between the body and the mind. When these two are out of synch, disease occurs. For too long body and mind have been erroneously treated as two separate units completely independent from one another.

The brain maintains perfect body temperature, synchronizes the heartbeat with the pulmonary rhythms, and performs many other miraculous functions without us being conscious of it.

The brain executes these functions using two components simultaneously. The nervous system executes certain tasks with the use of electricity, and the lymphatic system accomplishes the same objective by using chemicals produced by the glands. Either way, things get done.

If you are physically able, seriously consider martial arts as a form of exercise. This accomplishes two goals: because it involves the whole of the body, you will exercise muscles you did not even know you had. Also, there is a very spiritual side to the martial arts, and if you have a good instructor you will learn the virtue and honor of a true warrior.

If for some reason you decide that martial arts is too intense, or your body just isn't capable of dealing with it, try yoga. This will address the same objective, treating the brain as a muscle that if not used will wither away, just like physical muscles. There are many yogas. Find the one(s) that is right for you; but remember, those that require physical activity are best advised.

Yoga:
The Magick
of the East

Though reading and conversation
may furnish us with many ideas of
men and things, yet it is our own
meditation must from our judgment.
                    —Dr. I. Watts

*M*agick is the yoga of the West. The goal is the same, but the methods are slightly different. The main groups of yoga are:

1. **Hatha Yoga** = Health yoga, bringing the nerves to a calm state

2. **Raja Yoga** = Mental yoga, concentrative

3. **Nana Yoga** = Yoga of Knowledge

4. **Karma Yoga** = Yoga of work (karma comes from the Sanskrit word *kri,* which means "to do.")

5. **Bhakti Yoga** = Yoga of devotion, to see God in all things

6. **Mantra Yoga** = Yoga of speech

7. **Dhyani Yoga** = Yoga of meditation

8. **Kundalini Yoga** = Yoga of the life force

9. **Tantra Yoga** = Sexual yoga

The object of yoga is to stop all mental processes including itself. Yoga is the art of unity and love. When object and subject are united, knowledge occurs.

The process of yoga is as follows:

1. **Dharana** (fixing the mind on an object)

2. **Dhyana** (uniting object and subject)

3. **Samadhi** (the result of uniting object and subject; union with God)

4. **Samyama** (the result and accomplishment of all of the above)

There are eight ways in which the magician can achieve Samyama:

1. **Yama*** = Control, restraint

2. **Niyama*** = Restraint of the mind

---

*The object of these two is to stop all emotion or passion from disturbing the mind. It is probable that these practices were adopted by Christianity and manifested themselves as celibacy.

3. **Asana** = Posture; "that which is firm and pleasant"; any posture which is "steady and easy"

4. **Pranayama** = Control of breath; a process whereby all impurities are thrown out of the body

5. **Pratya Hara** = General examination of thoughts which one wishes to control

6. **Dharana** = Fixing the mind on a single point whereby the impurities of the mind are thrown out

7. **Dhyana** = Uniting the object with the subject

8. **Samadhi** = The result of uniting object with subject; union with God

The Senses

We do not see things the way they are
but as we are.

—Jewish proverb

*M*ost people possess five senses: sight, touch, smell, hearing, and taste. These can be attributed to the five elements; hence they also find their place in the points of the pentagram.

There is a "sixth sense" that is believed to reside within us all. There is some indication that this sense is transmitted in the genes, because some strongly psychic people have had strongly psychic children. It is conceivable that this sense is made up of all the information sent to the brain by our other senses. They gather together in our subconscious mind to create a separate, independent sense which furnishes any missing data relative to any experience.

When we human beings were in the early stages of evolution (before the use of language), we possessed a very powerful form of telepathy. It was the only way which we could communicate with one another. As the use of language became more prominent, telepathy diminished and we slowly ceased to use it.

The use of the senses is an evolutionary process designed to help the species deal with problems. Most of the parts of the brain with which science is familiar are dedicated to the methodology of processing electrical signals sent by our senses.

If the percentage of the brain which is unused can be used as a scale with which to measure human evolution, it then becomes clear that as a species we've got a long way to go.

There are ways to exercise this forgotten "sixth sense" and regain its use. The method which I have used with great success has proved to be a wonderful way to do this. I call it "isolation." It is a form of sensory deprivation.

The method is quite simple: you isolate all of the senses but one by focusing all your attention on the particular one you have chosen. You accomplish this by doing everything possible to prevent stimuli from reaching the other senses.

You may notice, for example, that a blind man has an acute sense of hearing and touch, while a deaf man possesses an incredible sense of sight and smell. This is because the consciousness (energy) required to operate the lost sense has been diverted to the healthy ones, thus making it possible for the brain to divert the energy once used on the damaged faculty to the other senses.

Imagine how much we could heighten the senses by alternately depriving all of them! Deprivation of the five will surely make you aware of the sixth.

This is not a new method. Egyptian adepts would subject their students to a similar method by making them spend days inside of pyramids. There they would find no light, sound, odors, or tastes. This proved to be quite a dreadful experience to all but a few very well balanced individuals. Let me explain something which must be made clear: **When the brain is denied the stimuli from the senses it will improvise with data which has been stored in the subconscious. Visions, voices, flavors, and odors are not unusual when performing these experiments. It is even possible to feel things on one's skin. It would be foolish to attempt this work without having first become adept with the Lesser Banishing Pentagram Ritual and having prepared your mind and body with Pranayama.**

The single and most important objective of this exercise is to enhance the senses so much that you can take them with you on the astral plane, where you must exercise complete control over your astral body. Exploring the astral is a beautiful experience when you can see it. It is much more enjoyable when you can touch it, hear it, smell it, and taste it.

It is theorized that the astral and etheric bodies are made up of **ectoplasm;** only in rare cases can this be physically seen by others. The more of yourself that you bring into the astral, the denser, stronger, and more visible the astral body.

Another word of warning: **If at any time you hear, see, feel, or otherwise experience something unpleasant you must make it stop. The most effective way is the "Star Ruby." Remember: these impressions must be willed and must not be allowed to manifest until they are called into consciousness by the magician. It is also good to keep in mind that any image whatsoever is a projection of your own subconscious**

mind. It cannot exist any other way! These impressions, when properly understood, can lead to better knowledge of yourself, and of course this must always be your goal.

There are many things at your disposal which you can use to isolate your senses: earplugs, blindfolds, nose plugs, etc.

Because our skin is so sensitive to pressure, temperature, and pain, I recommend the use of a flotation tank. Asana works moderately well, but it is quite uncomfortable unless you have mastered it. There are places you can visit, where for a nominal fee you can spend some time in a flotation tank.

There are just as many things to enhance your senses: music, the sound of the wind blowing on the trees, or the sound of the birds at sunrise. The taste of fruit and the fragrances of nature. The texture of bark, earth, and rocks, or the softness and temperature of the air as it caresses your body. The coolness of the water and the heat of the sun.

When working with sight, start with a living thing such as a tree. Look at it; I mean *really* look at it. Notice the different shades of green and brown. Try to see its aura. Is it more visible on the trunk or on the leaves? Find the true beauty in all things that you encounter; they are there for your pleasure. Also, keep in mind that no two people ever see the same object in exactly the same light. You will soon realize how much we normally don't see and how much we take for granted! Do similar things with the other senses, always depriving all others besides the one you are working with. Keep records in your diary. After some time you will have trained your mind so that it will be able to fix its energy on one sense while depriving the others, all without the use of the tools mentioned above, and this will help you even on the physical plane.

We begin programming our senses at birth when we have very little experience in the physical plane; as a result, our limited knowledge feeds us false information. That is why the sages of ancient times always insisted that all is an illusion. To illustrate this point, try this experiment:

1. Take a glass of *hot* water and place it in front of you on your left side.

2. Take a glass of *cold* water and place it in front of you on your right side.

3. Take a glass of *room temperature* water and place it in front of you between the other two glasses.

4. Put the forefinger of your left hand in the hot water and keep it there (naturally you will feel heat).

5. Put the forefinger of your right hand in the cold water and keep it there (naturally you will feel cold).

6. Take both of your fingers out of the hot and cold glasses and put them both into the glass containing the water at room temperature.

The finger that was once cold will now feel hot, while the finger that was hot will now feel cold, even though the water they are now in is neither cold nor hot. This experience is an illusion.

This is why we have to reprogram our senses, using the knowledge we have today. The exercise above will help to accomplish this.

There is yet another illusion that we face on a daily basis: *The illusion of color.*

When we look at a tree, we see the color green in its foliage because that is the color that is reflected by the leaves. This means that all the other colors except for green have been absorbed. In reality you are not seeing the tree, but a reflection of the tree. Everything we see is **Light.** We perceive light in the same manner that radar perceives sound, except that instead of picking up noise being bounced off of objects we pick up light being reflected from them. The true color of the leaves on the tree must then be every other color except green (which is not being absorbed but reflected).

By working with color wheels and using a little imagination, we can "train our brain" to pick up the true colors. Once we see the true essence of things we have overcome the illusion. (We see things for what they are. This process is what the alchemists call "the **First Matter.**")

Meditation

Without going outside, you may know the world. Without looking through the window, you may see the ways of heaven. The farther you go, the less you know. Thus the sage knows without traveling; He sees without looking; He works without doing.

—*Tao Te Ching*

W*ebster's New Collegiate Dictionary* defines "meditation" as:

1. "To focus one's thoughts on: reflect on or ponder over"

2. "To plan or project in the mind: to engage in contemplation or reflection"

Miguel de Molinos, a Catholic priest who lived in Italy in the 17th century, wrote that there were two kinds of prayer: outward prayer, which meant you physically pray with your voice, and inward prayer, which Molinos preferred over the other.

This inward prayer involved sitting in a quiet space and contemplating God. This angered church officials because Molinos' preaching could be interpreted to mean that confession to a priest was not really necessary if one confessed to God Himself using inward prayer. As a result Miguel became very popular with the people of that era. He became somewhat of a hero because his teachings attempted to liberate the people from the Church, which tried to oppress them and used confession as a tool for blackmail.

Miguel de Molinos was jailed for life by the Church, his book was banned, and anyone caught reading his book was to be excommunicated, all because he wrote that inward prayer was more efficient than outward prayer. The inward prayer Molinos spoke about was meditation.

To meditate, all you have to do is contemplate an object and hold it in consciousness for as long as it is desired. The mind will start to recall all data having anything to do with the object being contemplated, and by careful analysis of this data you can get deeper meanings of the object. Stress is reduced, it creates nerves of steel, and it increases concentration. So you see, it's not as hard as most people think. Or is it?

It is perfectly normal for the mind to rebel when you try to restrain it. If this does not happen at first, you are not doing it right! When this occurs allow the mind to run amuck for as long as it wants to. Eventually, (after about six or seven 15-minute sessions) you will start to notice that the random symbols the mind used to overwhelm you with at first have slowed down. Persevere until you can focus your attention on the chosen object for at least 15 minutes without interruption; then you are almost there.

It is extremely valuable if the first object you start with is one which you have a lot of interest in. This will make it easier for you to maintain focus on it. See Practical Exercises, page 135.

Magical Formulae

The spirit is the master, imagination
the tool, and the body the plastic
material.

—Paracelsus

*T*he basic principles for Magical Ritual are as
follows:

1. **Intent**—Decide what you want to accomplish.

2. **Classification**—Find the Sephiroth to best
encompass the intent.

3. **Research**—Look up the attributions to the Sephiroth in *Liber 777 and Other Qabalistic Writings of Aleister Crowley* (Samuel Weiser, 1986).

4. **Preparation**—Set up your temple, incense, oils, and weapons. Bathe and don your robe.

5. **Banish**—Perform the Lesser Banishing Ritual of the Pentagram and the Lesser Banishing Ritual of the Hexagram.

6. **Conjure**—Conjure the proper God using the Greater Hexagram Ritual.

7. **Transformation**—Assume that God form. Embody all of the characteristic properties of that God. Become it.

8. **Invoke**—Invoke the archangelic and planetary influences connected with the Sephiroth.

9. **Command**—Command the archangelic and planetary forces to bring the desired effect and demand its completion. (This must be done only when you are certain that the transformation has occurred successfully.)

10. **Banish and End**—Banish using the Lesser Banishing Pentagram and Hexagram Rituals. Avoid lust of result: assure yourself of the success of the operation and forget about it.

Ritual Timing

Time is the chrysalis of eternity.
                                    —Richter

*F*or the most part, practicing magicians place very little emphasis on timing, with the exception of the phases of the Sun and Moon. However, there is great folly in ignoring the rhythm of time. Much research confirms the fact that cycles *do* occur throughout the day. For example:

Until 1960, when Caesarean births became the preferred method of delivery, 65% of all births occurred between 4:00 and 6:00 AM.

Surveys have shown that the awareness level in most people reaches its peak at 12:00 AM, when the Sun is at its zenith.

Awareness plays such an important part in ceremonial
magick that the practitioner should become conscious of
which times of the day enable the best performance. This is
one of the functions of the diary.

Aside from performing rituals when the appropriate
planet is visible, there *are* no rules regarding timing. However,
it has been said elsewhere in this book that in magick you
must surround yourself with every possible characteristic that
your subconscious will recognize as a quality of the planet you
are working with. Therefore, by attributing timing to planetary elements, you add another symbol to your arsenal. I work
within the following guidelines:

1. Because of the strong magnetic field around the Earth,
    it is best to wait until at least 24 hours after the New
    Moon before doing invocations. Any time before or
    after this 24-hour period following the New Moon is
    okay. However, the best times for invocations are
    when the Moon is reflecting the most sunlight.

2. It is best to do your rituals on the days that correspond
    to the planet. For example:

    Monday corresponds to.........Luna
    Tuesdays corresponds to........Mars
    Wednesday corresponds to....Mercury
    Thursday corresponds to.......Jupiter
    Friday corresponds to ....Venus
    Saturday corresponds to........Saturn
    Sunday corresponds to ....Sun

3. It's best to do a planetary ritual when the concerned
    planet is either in conjunction with the Sun or when
    the planet is on the horizon. In general, be conscious
    of where the planets are at any given time.

4. Pick a day for rest. Fast if possible on that day. Burn incense to your Holy Guardian Angel or light a candle in His or Her honor, or perform some other form of devotion. "Inflame thyself in prayer."

The Psyche

> The mind is a mysterious form of matter secreted by the brain. Its chief activity consists in the endeavor to ascertain its own nature, the futility of the attempt being due to the fact that it has nothing but itself to know itself with.
> —Ambrose Bierce

*T*he psyche is made up of three different parts of consciousness which reside within the brain. In most people these parts work independently, unless they are forced to work together as a result of some form of psychological trauma. They have highly specialized functions, and once they are understood, can be taught to work together to create a more complete and efficient individual. The three parts are:

1. **The Conscious Mind** is symbolized as "The Magician" Tarot card. It is the rational mind, which in most of us operates normally during our waking hours. It is the reasoning mind. It is the state in which we *enter* our meditations. It draws "edited" information from the subconscious in an effort to make rational decisions based on past experiences. If there is ever any discrepancy between the subconscious and the conscious mind, the subconscious always wins.

2. **The Subconscious Mind** is symbolized by "The High Priestess" Tarot card. The function of the subconscious is primarily a defense mechanism. It functions always, without rest, but it is most prominent while we sleep. It stores all information and experience, but does not allow all of its data to be used by the *conscious* mind. It works without any effort on our part. It will take any suggestion, sort out all of the possibilities, and draw conclusions based on those suggestions, even if the suggestion is false.

   It is important to remember that the subconscious cannot be ordered; an indirect route is required. The subconscious is better reached by way of symbols. Some words are not allowed to enter into the subconscious realm. If words are used in a suggestion, one must never use words such as: *no, not,* and *never.* If you give yourself a suggestion such as "I will not smoke," the subconscious will remove the word "no" before it stores the suggestion, and it will store the words "I will smoke."

   All suggestions must be given without lust of result, or the subconscious will interpret the suggestion as an order and rebel against you. The subconscious is the place we *pass through* in our meditations.

3. **The Superconscious** is symbolized by "The Fool" Tarot card. It is the higher unconscious, the source of *all* consciousness. This is where the Higher Self is supposed to reside, the home of the deity within, the palace of the Holy Guardian Angel. This is the House of God, the place we *seek* in our meditations.

The brain should be looked on as a "receiver" which is capable of tuning in to the proper "thought wave." It can be conditioned to tune to higher forms of thought waves. The conditioning of the brain is the *goal* of our meditations.

The home of the sixth sense is in the right side of the brain, which is nonresistant in right-handed people. It is speculated that the brain's right side digests incoming stimuli and compares it against already stored information.

These impulses are stored a lot like the information on videotape, using images and symbols rather than text. The comparative process is instantaneous and is estimated to occur within about one-tenth of a second.

The left side of the brain consults with the right, and the result of a match is a feeling that "you've been here before," or "I know this guy," or "I know how this works."

This function of the brain has the power to generate a complete thought form, even though it is blurred by inadequate data. If there is no reference regarding an object or situation, the brain improvises (see "Courage," pages 37–8). Because it is a highly visual process, it is strongly linked with our emotional triggers. Hence the "gut feeling."

This function's main purpose is to create order from chaos; it puts experiences and information in their proper place, then executes a series of "experiments" in order to predict an outcome.

This is why those who have a strong awareness of this function are more likely to develop an accurate method by which to utilize this situation to its fullest. The magician sharpens this mechanism by using yoga, meditation, sensory deprivation, and similar disciplines.

The sixth sense can command with authority, even though it can at times be wrong. Do not let what seems to be failure in this function lead you to drop it or disregard it. It could save your life.

From the beginning of our lives, we have been trained to disregard this sixth sense. In fact, as children, many of us have been punished for following our instincts. Over time, man has all but evolved out of this primal function.

If you sense something about a person you don't like, listen to your intuition. This should not automatically close your mind to getting to know the person; in fact, the subconscious will insist on overwhelming evidence that there is nothing wrong with him or her.

As you study the magical arts, your "right brain" will be fed a tremendous number of symbols, pictures, and principles. It will sort them out, put them into the right sequence, and store them as video-like images to be recalled when the need arises. Symbols are ingenious keys by which we can access stored crucial information.

We have learned to shrug off this primal instinct of survival, yet it is a crucial part of all geomancy. We must now learn to bring back what society has forced us to disregard as delusion and psychosis.

Here is a simple formula with which we can communicate with the psyche to attain a desired result. It should be used in conjunction with the magical formulae:

1. **Intent**—Decide the purpose of the meditation and suggestion.

2. **Classification**—Find the Sephiroth to best encompass your desire.

3. **Preparation**—Use everything at your disposal related to the Sephiroth to inundate your senses with the essence of your desire. For example, use things like incense, fruits, and music.

4. **Presentation**—Delineate a symbol using the color and any other information you acquired during the classification that is best suited to convey your desire to the subconscious mind. (See *Practical Sigil Magic* by Frater U.˙.D.˙., Llewellyn Publications, 1990. This is an excellent source of information on how to design and "charge" sigils.)

5. **Pranayama**—In a relaxed state, situate your body in any position that is rigid but comfortable. Start your controlled breathing.

6. **Visualization**—Bring up the symbol you have designed to consciousness and hold it there. *Do not allow your mind to wander;* remember that the subconscious mind is watching. Hold this mental image for as long as it is comfortable.

7. **Affirmation**—Assure yourself that every picture you bring to your subconscious will be carried out.

8. **Forget About It!** Your subconscious must be allowed to take the ball and run with it. Any apprehension, skepticism, or anticipation will be decoded as "lust of result" and interfere with the process. Let the High Priestess handle it from here on. Do not allow lust of result to enter into the picture. This procedure can be used in conjunction with the technique laid out in "Magical Formulae," pages 113–4.

The Robe, the Altar, the Diary, and the Holy Oil

All ceremonies are, in themselves, very silly things; but yet a man of the world should know them. They are the out-works of manners and decency, which would be too often broken in upon, if it were not for that defense, which keeps the enemy at a proper distance. It is for this reason that I always treat fools and coxcombs with great cere-mony: true good breeding not being a sufficient barrier against them.

—Chesterfield

*M*uch nonsense has been written about how and where to acquire the materials for magical implements. One could become very discouraged if one tried to follow the

instructions in some of the medieval literature. The rational-
ity behind making this task so difficult is based on the premise
that the more work you put into these tools, the more detail
the subconscious mind will absorb about the object. These
objects are animated by virtue of focus and contemplation to
a level that they become an extension of the magician, a living
thing. To match the level of this integration, those who pur-
chase their implements will have to spend several months,
maybe even years, meditating on their tools.

This process need not be a tedious one; it is enough that
one refrain from purchasing a ready-made tool. Don't worry
if you do not feel capable of undertaking this seemingly
tedious task. Given enough time, magick will stimulate and
free the creative child within.

Remember that these implements are physical representations of your spiritual life. You should treat them with respect.
Once they have been consecrated to the Great Work, they
should not be handled by any other person. They are not toys;
treat them with reverence and they will be of great service. If
you feel inclined to show them off to your friends, read the
chapter on "Silence," pages 43–6.

The four elemental weapons (Wand, Cup, Dagger, and
Pentacle) embody four parts of the psyche depicted by the
four elements: Fire, Water, Air, and Earth (or if you prefer,
Yod-Heh-Vav-Heh: Tetragrammaton). They also allude to the
four planes of existence: Atziluth (the archetypal plane), Briah
(the creative plane), Yetzirah (the formative plane), and
Assiah (the material plane).

THE WAND

The Wand is the material depiction of the creative principles
of the magician. In short, it is a symbol or token of his or her
Will. Thus, to illustrate certitude and unshakable determina-
tion, it should be as straight as an arrow. It governs the ele-

ment of Fire and expresses the abstract process inherent in the plane of Atziluth.

There are many styles and variations of the Wand, especially in Golden Dawn temples, where every officer has a wand or scepter to illustrate a specific idea or principle. But here, we will only concern ourselves with the personal weapons of the solo magician.

Since in many ways the Wand can be compared to the phallus, many magicians go to great lengths to make their Wand in the same proportions as the physical organ it represents. The Wand is a symbol for the Hebrew letter Yod (׳), the Father, or Chokmah (Knowledge). Since copper is the metal attributed to Venus, or Netzach (Victory) on the Tree of Life, most fashion the Wand from this alloy in order to allude to the prolific aspects of the Work; "Love is the law, love under will."

For the implement to be useful it must be comfortable, and it should not demand attention which would otherwise be focused on the ritual. For a wooden Wand, I have found eight inches to be a comfortable length, with a width between $3/4$ and 1 inch. For a solid copper Wand a diameter of $1/2$ inch is sufficient. After it is consecrated, keep it in a red silk bag.

THE CUP

The Cup is the physical object which portrays the element of Water. As the Wand represents the magician's Will, the Cup personifies his or her Understanding. It illustrates the methodology of the plane of Briah.

The Cup as a symbol represents a female idea; hence it is associated with the yoni (the archetypal vagina). The Cup is a symbol of the Hebrew letter Heh (ה), the Mother. Since it represents Understanding, or Binah on the Tree of Life, it is only appropriate that the diameter be three inches. Silver is the rightful alloy for this instrument, which signals to the Moon, or Yesod (Foundation) on the Tree of Life. It should be deep enough to hold wine without easily spilling it when one moves about.

The message behind the Cup illustrated by Yesod and Binah is that the Understanding of the Magician is as deep as the waters we call our subconscious; it has a deeper significance than day-to-day understanding. After it is consecrated, store it in a blue silk bag.

THE DAGGER

The Dagger is an animation of the element of Air. It is symbolized on the Tree of Life by Tiphareth (Beauty), and its planet is the Sun. The Dagger is a symbol for the Hebrew letter Vav (ו), the Son. It explains the process of Yetzirah (the formative plane), and symbolizes the intellectual capacity of the Magician (the reason).

Most practitioners of the Art treat the Dagger as a Martian implement which dictates judicial authority over demons. This is a job best fulfilled by the Sword, a more advanced implement, and will not be discussed in this treatise. The Dagger is uniquely Air; unlike the Sword it threatens malignant spirits with intelligence rather than force.

The blade should be double-edged, with a length of about eight inches in order to embody the intellectual properties of the Mercurial Sephiroth; Hod, Science.

Since human beings have a tendency to accept only principles that endorse what they believe to be "reason," make the hilt from the Venusian alloy copper to balance the illusion of intellectual superiority. The correspondences of copper are best embodied by the Sephirah Netzach, Art. It is a gentle reminder that magick is both the science *and* art of causing change to occur in conformity with Will. After the Dagger is dedicated to the Work, keep it in a yellow silk bag.

THE PENTACLE

The Pentacle also corresponds to the Hebrew letter Heh (ה). It is a symbol of Earth, and it represents the body of the magician, the house of God. It is the magician's sustenance. It exhibits the traits of the plane of Assiah. It is the Daughter.

The Pentacle should be made of beeswax with a diameter of 8 inches and a thickness of $1/2$ inch. Upon the surface, the magician should carve an image that describes the *whole* of the universe. Nothing should be left out. The whole idea here is to reduce all of those things which the magician perceives as the universe to a minuscule dot. The design need not be as elaborate as Dr. John Dee's; symbols which allude to similar ideas can be combined in order to reduce the amount of detail. But it is important that it be complete. When you are done, you will know.

This, of course, may take much meditation, so you should take your time with this implement to avoid having to do this twice. The Pentacle will reflect the magician's subconscious perception of the universe. Once it has been blessed, safeguard it in green silk.

THE ROBE

The Robe is the armor of the Magician. It should be loose fitting and comfortable, and it should be of a material which is light, soft, and capable of breathing. Cotton is a good material. So is a poly\cotton blend. However, wool is the best because of its ability to direct astral energy.

The color is really a matter of personal choice. One should try to match the color as closely as possible to the Sephiroth being worked with. This would, however, require that the magician keep ten different Robes, one for each Sephirah. For this reason most magicians use black Robes.

Black is the accumulation of all colors and is therefore appropriate for any working. It is so neutral that it is not likely to distract you in the middle of your Work. Furthermore, black absorbs color; it attracts light by behaving like a solar panel and should be used for any ritual designed to fortify the aura, such as the Pentagram Ritual, Middle Pillar, etc.

White, on the other hand is the absence of all color. It repels light, which makes a great shield and should be used when working with hostile forces. I have one of each.

Whether or not to have a hood is also a personal preference. I favor a hooded Robe because it allows me to feel completely shielded, but some would argue that a hood is distracting because it shifts about on your head.

Whether you make your Robe hooded, and whatever color you decide is best for you, remember that the garment should be loose and comfortable. You should never wear any underclothes while wearing your Robe. Wide sleeves look great, but they are in danger of catching fire should you lean over your Altar candles. A zipper may be practical, but you will feel it rub against your skin. The fewer distractions, the better the Robe.

THE ALTAR

The Altar is composed of a double cube. The bottom cube represents the underlying force of the Great Work; Love. The top cube represents the Will of the magician. "Love is the law, love under will," or "As above, so below," and further: "Kether is in Malkuth, and Malkuth in Kether, but after another manner."

There need not be a division between both cubes. In fact, if it is made as a single, unseparated rectangular unit, you can use it to store your implements.

The Altar should be 36" high, 18" wide, and 18" deep. It should be black on the outside to illustrate the *accumulation* of all colors and white on the inside to depict the *absence* of all color. Plywood or particle board are perfect. The thickness of the wood should be taken into consideration; a heavy Altar will need hidden wheels under it to make it easier to move around. A lighter Altar will not support much weight.

Once the Altar is finished, it can be painted. I have seen one that was covered in veneer; black on the outside and white on the inside. This move proved to be worth the extra effort, as the surface is virtually stain-proof, it tolerates the heat generated by the incense burner, and wax from candles peels right off.

One side of the Altar should be a door with hidden hinges and a lock. The inside should have a shelf for *The Book of the Law*, incense, charcoal, burner, Pentacle, Cup, candles, and holders. There should be a place to hang the Wand and Dagger.

THE HOLY OIL

The anointing oil of the Magician should metaphorically represent the desire of the Holy Guardian Angel to join with its lower counterpart, the magician. All of the being, temple, and weapons should be consecrated and anointed with this oil. With this in mind, one should take care to only use the highest quality oils available.

During the Aeon of the Sacrificial Gods, the oil used to embody the current of the times was "Jerusalem Oil." This was simply composed of equal portions of frankincense and myrrh, both traditionally used in burial ceremonies.

The fragrance mentioned above is dated, and the New Aeon magician should resort to an essence which best depicts the joy and strength of the Age of the Child. The following is a formula for such an oil. It is named after its creator, the 17th-century magician, Abramelin.

In a glass vessel mix four parts cinnamon oil, two parts myrrh oil, one part galangal oil, and seven parts olive oil.

If fine oils are used in the proper proportions, the mixture should have a clear, golden appearance. It should tingle slightly. If it stings, it can be diluted by adding more olive oil, but you should only resort to this if it causes serious discomfort. Now for a word of warning: *cinnamon oil is very caustic.* If you keep your oil in a plastic bottle it may melt and ruin your Altar or some other thing that you have devoted a great deal of time to. Use only glass receptacles.

THE DIARY

The magical Diary should only contain data pertinent to magick, that is; everything. Every entry should start with the date, time, year, and solar and lunar positioning. It should contain all of your feelings, what you ate that day, the weather, etc. A lot of these things may not sound important now, but believe me, if you are trying to duplicate an experiment it will be necessary to recreate all of the elements which may have played a role in the original operation.

For this reason, take care to chose words that convey your message as clearly as possible. Writing in code may add to the romance and mystery associated with magick, but if your Diary does not convey enough information to reproduce experiments, then all is lost.

Since the days of the week are representations of the seven ancient planets, it is handy to write the planetary symbol associated with the day of the week instead. For example:

Monday............................Luna ☽

Tuesdays...........................Mars ♂

Wednesday.......................Mercury ☿

Thursday..........................Jupiter ♃

Friday..............................Venus ♀

Saturday...........................Saturn ♄

Sunday.............................Sun ☉

The following is an example of a thoroughly composed diary entry.

♂ August 11th, 1992 e.v. ~ 11:30 p.m.

☉ in ♋ , ☽ in ♑

6:30 a.m. Awoke, ☌☉ Solar Adoration. Ate fruit for breakfast.

7:30 a.m. Lesser Banishing Ritual of the Pentagram & Hexagram.

8:30 a.m. Off to work in great spirits.

12:00 noon Ate light lunch of vegetables and cheese. Solar Adoration in bathroom at work. Felt energized.

6:00 p.m. Home from work.

6:30 p.m. Ate dinner ~ glass of wine, leg of chicken and steamed vegetables and rice. Solar Adoration.

7:00 p.m. Practiced Prana-yama in Dragon Asana with four-fold breath. Legs began to fall asleep within 5 minutes. Visualized apple, mind wandered slightly at first, but quieted down within 2 or 3 minutes. Lesser Banishing Ritual of the Pentagram.

8:00 p.m. Began writing my life story.

9:00 p.m. Read Raja Yoga by Swami Vivekananda until 11:00.

11:30 p.m. Solar Adoration, then went to bed.

Page from a Magical Diary

Practical
Exercises

EXERCISE
IN MEDITATION

*L*et's suppose you have chosen an apple, as I did many years ago, as your first subject/object of focus.

- Sit in a comfortable Asana and start relaxing your body, quieting your thoughts and regulating your breathing. Keep in mind that you have to be able to relax in order to meditate.

- When you have stilled your mind and body, try to visualize a shiny bright red apple against a black background.

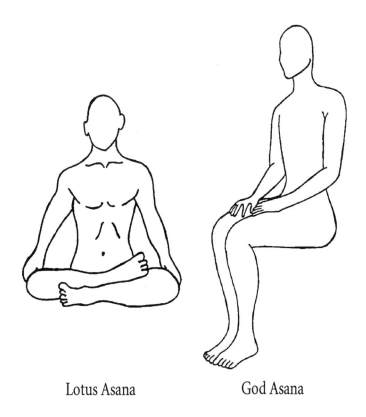

Lotus Asana   God Asana

- Focus on it and bring it closer so that you can pay attention to the detail on its skin.

- Try to smell it.

- Try to feel it.

- Try to bite it and taste it.

In short, try to experience the object fully. Unite with it. All of this takes place in your mind. The next step, once the inner senses have had their fun with the object, is to allow your mind to recall data related to the object. Study and analyze each one, but keep your third eye always focused on the object. If you allow your "vision" to drift to another theme while you are analyzing data, your mind will recall symbols connected with the current theme and you will mix the symbols. Do not allow this to happen! Purity of thought means not allowing the mind to drift from one symbol to another unless the symbols are somehow connected.

The union of object with object comes much later in your magical training. The first step is the union of subject with object.

It is easy to become discouraged during this phase of training, but I cannot find the words to convey how important this Work is.

A few tips to make things easier for you:

- Do not meditate lying down. If you become bored you will fall asleep. If you do this a lot it will become a conditioned reflex so that every time you attempt to meditate you will sleep instead.

- In the beginning fix your attention on only those things which interest you. It is easier to occupy the mind on things it finds pleasant. I find the Tarot to be so full of esoteric symbolisms that for me it is the best training aid I can recommend. I suggest the deck illustrated by Frieda Harris under the instruction of Aleister Crowley. The colors are superb and the pictures have a positive effect on the psyche. Later, when you have sufficient control over your thoughts, move on to harder objects.

- Whenever possible begin your meditations after midnight. The world sleeps, and the psychic interference which is present when others are worrying about making it to work on time, making money, paying bills, and keeping their wits about them in the mundane world won't be there to disrupt your Work.

- Some people recommend the use of a mantra. If you are going to use one of these make sure that your mantra does not become so ingrained into consciousness that it becomes the object of all of your meditations. Sometimes these habits are hard to break. The mantra *AOM* is the most popular. The object of the mantra is twofold: for most people it is an audible form of focus. What most people don't realize is that it also stimulates certain parts of the brain by vibrating the bones of the head. People who have used mantra swear by it; I personally believe that it silences the internal dialogue.

- The Lesser Ritual of the Pentagram is specifically made to create an area in which to Work. You may want to do one of these before and one after meditating.

- In the beginning, try to feel about meditation as you felt as a child when opening gifts on your birthday. Once you have overcome the obvious obstacles to meditation, you will be enthusiastic enough not to need any other reason to meditate other than the pleasant feeling associated with it.

- Don't give up until you reach that point. It does not take as long as you may think to become proficient at this. I have seen people showing all the obvious signs of success just to watch them give up the practice *right before they achieve their goal!* If they only knew how close they were they would have never given up.

Remember: in magick we subject our minds, bodies, and nervous systems to extraordinary energy levels. Meditation prepares us for the journey by disciplining our minds. For this reason the ability to meditate is probably one of the most important parts of our Work. It may one day allow you to communicate and look into the eyes of your God.

The following is a very advanced meditation I have been working on for several years. It is printed solely for the purpose of illustrating more advanced methods of contemplation and is not intended for the beginner. You may want to try this once you have mastered fixing the mind on an object and uniting with it until nothing else in the universe exists except for that object. Obviously, if you desire a male consort you should make the necessary alterations to this meditation.

THE ASTRAL TEMPLE

Build yourself a castle in a tranquil place in your mind. It should be made from square stone. It should be surrounded by water and be equipped with a drawbridge that must open and close at will. The chain for the mechanism of the drawbridge you must forge yourself. Know every link in that chain.

The dwelling should have a master's quarters, a stable for your fine stallions, a servants' room, a meeting place where you and your knights can discuss battle plans, a furnace for forging, a kitchen also made from rock, and rooms for your knights' squires and guests.

Brick by brick, stone by stone, you must build this castle, taking time to remember each brick as it was cut and laid down, its texture, weight, etc. Smell the mortar, remember its consistency. This will take much effort at first, for it requires a great deal of concentration and planning. You must remember everything, so that when you withdraw from this meditation you are able to return to it and pick up where you left off.

You will tire after a while, but I assure you that if you continue this meditation to its completion you will find that it was not just a mere exercise in concentration.

There is no time limit on this; it could take a lifetime to finish this Work alone. The important thing is not to leave the Work until it is completed.

When you have finished with this abode, you must assign a King to it, as noble, powerful, and wise as you could ever hope to be if you were King of this kingdom yourself. He must be a compassionate man. He will be ruler, judge, priest, warrior, and magician.

Dress him in fine silks, gold, and rubies. Give him power over the castle and the land wherein he dwells. He must be a great leader, an adept in weaponry and master of all he does. Forge for him a beautiful sword, and equally beautiful armor.

Create for him a beautiful woman, with eyes as green as the calm seas. She will be his Queen. Dress her also in fine silks, gold, and rubies. She must possess the same inner qualities as her husband King.

Fill the castle with brave warriors, skilled in their art, and give them chainmail and armor forged by the blacksmiths of the kingdom.

Design a crest of gold, silver, and diamonds, all in a background of lapis lazuli. The crest must symbolically express your inner nature, your love for freedom, your loyalty to your brethren, and your aspiration to your God. Next, make banners and mantles from this crest and give it to your army, that they shall wear it above their armor in reverence to their King and Queen. Place this crest in the temple, in the King's chamber, in the meeting places for his knights, and in the eating places.

You must be a fair King; see to it that you are kind to your servants and give your people whatever they need, so that they shall want not, just as our Lord the Sun provides for all who revolve around Him.

Build your Kingdom on a solid foundation, consisting of intelligence, devotion, balance, strength, mercy, understanding, and wisdom. You must possess all these things within before you can put on that golden white crown which will one day make you King.

ASTRAL TRAVEL

As stated earlier, meditation is merely the ability to remember and re-experience specific details communicated by our senses.

Astral travel, on the other hand, is the talent to journey *inward*, and using the abilities mentioned above, to create a space and circumstance whereby the mental body can experience a separate reality independent from the physical body.

During this "transfer of consciousness," the mental (astral) body must be allowed to collect data sent through the senses. In other words, once the separation has taken place, the astral body must be able to see, feel, hear, smell, and taste the new world it is exploring.

The following exercises will help to get you started:

Choose a quiet evening and a familiar room where you are not likely to be interrupted. Remember that you must be "passively active," so don't try it when you are very tired or you might fall asleep.

- Look around you and take a mental photograph of your surroundings.

- Lay on your back and take a deep breath to help you relax. Loosen all of your muscles, especially your neck.

- Close your eyes and recall your surroundings by bringing the mental photograph to consciousness. This may take some time, but do not progress until you can do this for several minutes. If you have difficulty you must spend more time practicing the meditation steps listed above.

- Once you have formulated this image (with your physical eyes closed), focus your attention at the space directly in front of your feet with your mind's eye.

- The conscious is the paint, the subconscious is the canvas, and the artist is the Self. Imagine a cloaked figure standing at your feet wearing a black, hooded robe. Hold the image as long as you can. It is normal to see it fading in and out, but persist until it remains as solid as the rest of the images around you. Focus your attention on the hood.

- Once you have completed *all* of these steps, shift your consciousness to the robed figure. Your mind will fight you at first, and glimpses from within the hood will flicker back and forth from both bodies; you may receive sensory input from two places. This is normal; do not feel discouraged.

- After some practice, you will be able to "jump" into that robed figure. When you do, you will be able to see your body lying before you. *Don't panic,* or you will bounce right back into your body. People have reported being able to "see" 360 degrees once they have occupied the astral robe.

- Once you are in, and can remain inside for long periods of time, walk around. Touch the walls until you can feel their texture. Pass your hand over the candles, feel the warmth. Smell the incense. Bring all of your senses into play in this practice.

- Walk in front of a mirror and pull back the hood; you should see yourself. Don't be alarmed if you don't look exactly as you do with your physical eyes; remember that sight is an illusion.

- After a few minutes, locate your physical body (it's right there lying on its back, remember?) and turn your back to it. Lie down on top of it until both images have blended together.

- Open your eyes, take a deep breath, and banish. Some people like to eat after this practice.

This practice sounds much more difficult than it really is. But once you start getting results it is very gratifying. Don't let failures discourage you from trying again some other time. Log both failures and triumphs into your diary; your subconscious may be trying to communicate something to you.

THE LESSER BANISHING RITUAL OF THE PENTAGRAM

We have already explained how the brain tunes in to a specific frequency. The Lesser Banishing Ritual of the Pentagram is a way to get the brain to change frequency. It does this by simply removing your attention from whatever you may be experiencing at that particular time and allowing you to focus your mind on other things. Thus, the original thought/experience has been banished.

This ritual is more of an invoking than a banishing, as you will realize when you start visualizing the archangels. Since the elements are attributed to the senses, there is an intimacy which exists between the archangels and parts of the psyche ruling them; thus, during this part of the ritual, the senses are being called to attention. This ritual provides three functions: To create a space in which to Work, to heighten your ability to perceive reality through the senses, and to stimulate the brain and kundalini through the use of Pranayama.

To illustrate the importance of this rite, Aleister Crowley once wrote: "Cleanliness is next to Godliness, and had better come first."

In order to facilitate things, we will break the ritual up into four parts: the Qabalistic Cross, the Pentagrams, the Invocation of the Kerubic Forces, and the Closing.

Part One: The Qabalistic Cross

In this segment of the ceremony you become the nucleus of your own universe by magically establishing pole and equator and then positioning your heart chakra at their intersection.

1. Face East. With the Sign of Benediction, touch your forehead and say **ATEH** (Hebrew form of "thou," attributed to Kether).

2. Touch your breast and say **AIWASS** (the herald of the New Aeon, attributed to Tiphareth on the Tree of Life; when your Holy Guardian Angel reveals Its name to you, substitute that name for Aiwass).

3. Touch your genital area and say **MALKUTH** (Hebrew word meaning "kingdom," attributed to Malkuth on the Tree of Life).

4. Touch your right shoulder and say **VE-GEBURAH** (Hebrew for "and the power," attributed to Geburah on the Tree of Life).

5. Touch your left shoulder and say **VE-GEDULAH** (Hebrew for "and the glory").

6. Cross your arms on your breast, left over right, composing the Sign of the Blazing Star, and say **LE-OLAHM, AMEN** (Hebrew for "to the ages, Amen").

(The Hebrew in this part of the ritual is the last part of the Lord's Prayer. The crossing of your arms over the breast symbolizes the Rose on the Cross.)

Part Two: The Pentagrams

The proper weapon for this rite is the Air Dagger, *not* the Sword. The Sword is a symbol of strength and force, useful for manipulating more advanced entities such as demons. The Air Dagger, being symbolic of the intellect of the magician, displays intellectual mastery over them.

Pranayama is introduced at this point of the ceremony in order to increase the amount of oxygen in the blood. When tracing the pentagrams, breathe in deeply with every line which moves up, exhale with every line that moves down, and hold your breath for the line that moves horizontally.

1. Advance to the East placing your right heel in the hollow of your left foot and construct the Pentagram of Earth with the proper weapon. (While constructing the Pentagram, remember to inhale deeply through your nose for the upward strokes and exhale slowly through your nose for the downward strokes. Retain the breath for the cross strokes). Visualize the Pentagram as it were blazing with radiant flames of Fire.

2. Advance your left foot 12 inches and throw your body forward. Let your hands (drawn back to the sides of your head) shoot out, so that you are standing in the Sign of the Enterer (see illustration). At the same time, stab the center of the Pentagram with the Dagger and vibrate **YOD-HEH-VAV-HEH** (Hebrew for "Jehovah") with forcible exaltation. Come back to an upright position in the Sign of Silence.

3. With the Dagger still uplifted, turn to the South and proceed as before, but vibrate **ADONI** (Hebrew for "Lord").

4. With the Dagger still uplifted, turn to the West and proceed as before, but vibrate **EHEIEH** (Hebrew for "I AM").

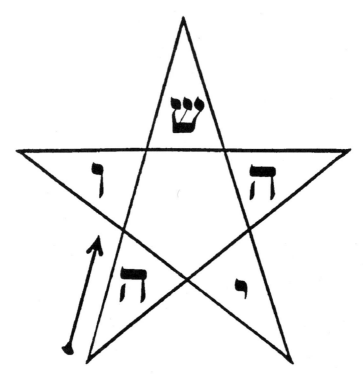

Banishing Earth Pentagram

5. With the Dagger still uplifted, proceed to the North and vibrate **ATEH GIBOR LE-OLAHM ADONI** (Hebrew for "To Thee be the Power unto the Ages, O Lord").

6. With the Dagger still uplifted, return to the East.

Part Three: The Invocation of the Kerubic Powers

It is probably evident by now that imagination is a key player in this event. Practice visualization until you can clearly see

Sign of the Enterer

the images and archangels. Also, in order to build your astral senses, it is important that you use them as much as possible in conjunction with your astral sight.

1. Stand in the Sign of Extended Light. Visualize an archangel before you wearing a yellow robe. Remember and re-create the physical feelings associated with having your body caressed by a warm summer breeze and say **BEFORE ME RAPHAEL** (try to feel the breeze coming from the East).

2. Visualize an archangel behind you wearing a violet robe. Remember and re-create the physical feelings associated with having the ocean spray coming from behind you and say **BEHIND ME GABRIEL.**

3. Visualize an archangel at your right side wearing a red robe. Remember and re-create the physical feelings associated with the heat of a fireplace warming the right side of your body and say **ON MY RIGHT HAND MICHAEL.**

4. Visualize an archangel at your left side wearing a black robe. Remember and re-create the physical feelings associated with the taste of an apple and say **ON MY LEFT HAND URIEL.**

5. Still in the Sign of Extended Light say **FOR ABOUT ME FLAME THE PENTAGRAMS, AND IN THE COLUMN SHINES THE SIX- RAYED STAR.**

Part Four: The Closing

1. Repeat the Qabalistic Cross.

2. Press your forefinger against your bottom lip.

3. Release your finger from your mouth and say **ABRA-HADABRA.**

LATIN VARIATION OF THE PENTAGRAM RITUAL

Since the Qabalistic Cross is actually the last part of the Lord's Prayer, and was commonly recited in Latin in Medieval Europe, I decided to include it here for the sake of giving the reader a variation of the ritual which is not commonly put into practice. The practitioner will notice that in Latin the whole rite feels like a completely different action, with a different purpose than that of its Hebrew counterpart. Try them both (on separate occasions) and record your findings, feelings, projections, thoughts, weather, etc., in your diary.

Part One: The Qabalistic Cross

1. Face East and with the Sign of Benediction touch your forehead and say **QUIA TUMM.**

2. Touch your heart and say **AIWASS.**

3. Touch your genital area and say **EST REGNUM.**

4. Touch your right shoulder and say **ET POTESTA.**

5. Touch your left shoulder and say **ET GLORIA.**

6. Cross your arms over the breast, left over right, composing the sign of the Blazing Star and say **IN SECULA AMEN.**

Part Two: The Pentagrams

1. Advance to the East, placing your right heel in the hollow of your left foot, and construct the Pentagram of Earth with the proper weapon. (While constructing the Pentagram, inhale deeply through your nose for

the upward strokes and exhale slowly through your nose for the downward strokes. Retain the breath for the cross stroke). Visualize the Pentagram as if it were blazing with radiant flames of Fire.

2. Advance your left foot 12 inches and throw your body forward. Let your hands (drawn back to the sides of the head) shoot out, so that you are standing in the Sign of the Enterer. At the same time, stab the center of the Pentagram with the Dagger and vibrate **DEO** (Latin for "God") with forcible exhalation. Come back to an upright position in the Sign of Silence.

3. With Dagger still uplifted, turn to the South and proceed as before, but vibrate **DOMINUS** (Latin for "Lord").

4. With the Dagger still uplifted, turn to the West and proceed as before, but vibrate **SUM** (Latin for "I AM").

5. With the Dagger still uplifted, turn towards North and vibrate **QUIA TUMM EST REGNUM ET POTESTA ET GLORIA, IN SECULA; AMEN.** (Latin for "To Thee be the Power unto the Ages, O Lord").

5. With the Dagger still uplifted, return to the East.

Part Three: The Invocation of the Kerubic Powers

1. Visualize an archangel before you wearing a yellow robe. Imagine a summer breeze that caresses your body as you say **PRO MEO RAPHAEL.**

2. Visualize an archangel behind you wearing a violet robe. Feel the mist of the ocean spray as you say **PONE MEO GABRIEL.**

3. Visualize an archangel at your right side wearing a red robe. See the eternal fires that blaze about in the hearts of men and say **AD DEXTRO MEO MICHAEL.**

4. Visualize an archangel at your left side wearing a black robe. Taste the fruits of the fertile Earth as you say **AD SINISTRO MEO URIEL.**

5. In silence use your inner voice and say **QUOD CIR-CUM MEUM PENTAGRAMA FLAMARE, ET COLUMNA STELLA SEXTUPLUS STARE LUCERE.**

Part Four: The Closing

1. Repeat the Qabalistic Cross.

2. Press your forefinger against your bottom lip.

3. Release your finger from your mouth and say **ABRA-HADABRA.**

THE LESSER BANISHING HEXAGRAM RITUAL

1. Stand facing East with your Wand at your breast and say:

   I. N. R. I.
   YOD, NUN, RESH, YOD.
   VIRGO, ISIS, HOLY MOTHER.
   SCORPIO, APOPHIS, HOLY FATHER.
   SOL, OSIRIS, SLAIN AND RISEN.
   ISIS, APOPHIS, OSIRIS.
   IAO.

2. Still facing East, formulate the Sign of Extended Light and say **THE SIGN OF OSIRIS SLAIN.**

3. Formulate the Sign of the Swastika and say **THE SIGN OF THE MOURNING OF ISIS.**

4. Formulate the Sign of Isa the Adorant and say **THE SIGN OF APOPHIS AND TYPHON.**

5. Formulate the Sign of the Blazing Star and say **THE SIGN OF OSIRIS RISEN.**

6. Formulate the sign in step 2 and follow it with the sign in step 3 as you say **L.V.X., LUX, THE LIGHT OF THE CROSS.**

7. Advance to the East and trace the unicursal Hexagram with your Wand, draw in your breath, throw your hands and body forward into the Sign of the Enterer and say **ABRAHADABRA.** Imagine the Hexagram shooting forth and a five-petaled rose blooming in the center.

8. Repeat to the South, West, and North.

9. Facing East, repeat steps 1 through 6.

LIBER XXV: THE STAR RUBY

This is absolutely a martial ritual, with the emphasis on the number five (Geburah). Unlike the Lesser Banishing Ritual of the Pentagram, the archangels are of a Chaldean origin. This one should be used to "get rid of" those things which are unwanted. This ritual should eventually be substituted for the Lesser Banishing Ritual of the Pentagram, as it is more effective and goes far beyond the elemental realm.

This Ritual is written in Greek. I have attempted to write it phonetically in order to simplify things for those of you who are not familiar with the Greek language. However, I strongly recommend that you learn the alphabet and its correspondences, as a great many Western holy books have been written in Greek.

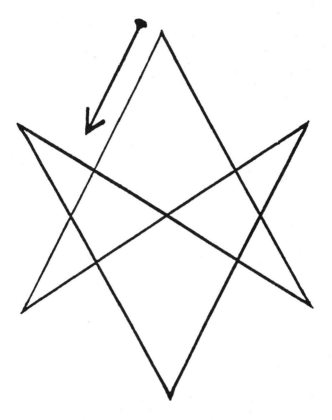

Banishing Solar (Unicursal) Hexagram

The Cross

1. Face East and inhale deeply. Press your right forefinger against your bottom lip.

2. Sweep your hand out and away from you, expelling forcibly the air and cry **APO PANTOS KAKODAYA-MANOS!** (Flee from me all evil spirits!)

The Sign of Osiris Slain
(Sign of Extended Light)

The Sign of Isis Mourning

The Sign of Typhon

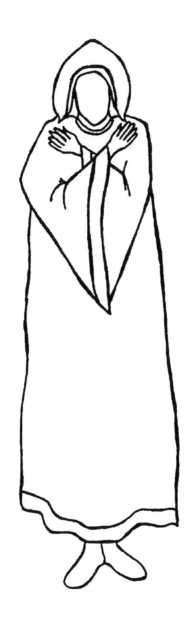

The Sign of Osiris Risen

3. Touch your forehead and say **SOY** ("Thou," same as *Ateh)*.

4. Touch your groin and say **O PHALLAE** (Phallus, Father, Man, Human, Creative Energy).

5. Touch your right shoulder and say **ISJUROS** (Strength, same as Geburah)

6. Touch your left shoulder and say **UJARISTOS** (Thanksgiving, same as Chesed, etc.)

7. Clasp your hands in front of you, interlocking your fingers, and cry **IAO** (Greek equivalent of IHVH).

The Pentagrams

1. Advance to the East and imagine a Pentagram flaming on your forehead. Perform the Sign of the Enterer and, as your hands pass by your eyes, fling forth the Pentagram and roar **THERION.**

2. Do the same thing in the North, but say **NUIT.**

3. Do the same thing in the West, but hiss **BABALON.**

4. Do the same thing in the South, but bellow **HADIT.**

5. Returning to the East and in the signs of N.O.X. sing **IO PAN.**

Posting the Guards

Extend your arms in the Sign of Extended Light and say lowly but clearly:

1. **PRO MU YUNGUS** ("Before me Jungus").

2. **OPPISO MU TELETARCHIE** ("Opposite me Teletarchie").

3. **EPIDEXIA SINOKIS** ("At my best hand Sinokis").

4. **EPIRRISTORA DIAMANOS** ("At my other hand Diamanos").

5. **FLENGAE GAR PERI MU HO ASTERTON PENTE** ("Flames all around me the Star of the Five").

6. **KAI EN TE STELLE HO ASTERTON HEX ESTEKI** ("In the column it stands the Star of the Six").

Repeat the cross.

PRANAYAMA: CONTROLLING THE BREATH

The fourfold breath.

1. Choose a rigid but comfortable position in which you are not likely to fall asleep.

2. Take in a few deep cleansing breaths, and clear your mind.

3. Place your right thumb against your right nostril so that it closes it off. Don't pinch; push.

3. After exhaling all of the air from your lungs, inhale through your left nostril for a count of four. By the time you reach four, your lungs should be filled to capacity. This may take some practice to develop a rhythm; pace yourself.

5. Hold for a count of four.

6. Move your thumb away from your right nostril and push your right forefinger against your left nostril. Exhale through your right nostril for a count of four.

Sign of Puella
(The Daughter)

ה

Sign of Puer
(The Son)

ר

Sign of Mulier
(The Mother)

ה

Sign of Vir
(The Father)

＇

7. Hold for a count of four.

8. Inhale through your right nostril for a count of four.

9. Hold for four counts.

10. Move your forefinger away from your left nostril and push your thumb against your right nostril. Exhale for four counts.

11. Repeat steps 1–10 for about 15 minutes.

After you get used to this exercise, it may become necessary to change the count to six, then eight, etc. I have found the use of a metronome invaluable. Just set it for a rhythm that feels comfortable.

LIBER RESH

This is a solar adoration which should be performed four times daily. The Sun has always represented the highest ideals of human consciousness: Godhood. Because the physical Sun is responsible for all life on the planet, it is easy to see why the ancients paid so much reverence to it. Most ancient texts (including the Bible) contain descriptions of God which are undeniably congruent with that of our Sun.

One of the many purposes of the following adoration is to serve as a constant reminder of that Light without which we would be nothing, and to encourage the practitioner to radiate that same Light to those in need.

At Sunrise, embrace the Sun in the East in the sign of the Blazing Star (arms crossed over the chest; right over left). In a loud voice say:

HAIL UNTO THEE WHO ART RA IN THY RISING, EVEN UNTO THEE WHO ART RA IN THY

STRENGTH, WHO TRAVELEST OVER THE HEAVENS IN THY BARK AT THE UPRISING OF THE SUN. TAHUTI STANDETH IN HIS SPLENDOR AT THE PROW, AND RA-HOOR ABIDETH AT THE HELM. HAIL UNTO THEE FROM THE ABODES OF NIGHT!

At Noon, welcome the Sun in the South in the sign of Fire (extend the fingers of both hands, joining the forefingers and thumbs so that they form a triangle. Place this triangle upon your forehead). In a loud voice say:

HAIL UNTO THEE WHO ART AHATHOOR IN THY TRIUMPHING, EVEN UNTO THEE WHO ART AHATHOOR IN THY BEAUTY, WHO TRAVELEST OVER THE HEAVENS IN THY BARK AT THE MID-COURSE OF THE SUN. TAHUTI STANDETH IN HIS SPLENDOR AT THE PROW, AND RA-HOOR ABIDETH AT THE HELM. HAIL UNTO THEE FROM THE ABODES OF MORNING!

At Sunset, greet the Sun in the West in the sign of the God Shu (both arms at right angles with the hands facing up slightly above the head, as if you were supporting something above your head). In a loud voice say:

HAIL UNTO THEE, WHO ART TUM IN THY SETTING, EVEN UNTO THEE WHO ART TUM IN THY JOY, WHO TRAVELEST OVER THE HEAVENS IN THY BARK AT THE DOWN-GOING OF THE SUN. TAHUTI STANDETH IN HIS SPLENDOR AT THE PROW, AND RA-HOOR ABIDETH AT THE HELM. HAIL UNTO THEE FROM THE ABODES OF DAY!

Finally, **at Midnight;** recognize the Sun in the North in the sign of Water (the tips of the thumbs and forefingers touching making a triangle. Place the triangle on the solar plexus so that the apex of the triangle is pointing down). In a loud voice say:

HAIL UNTO THEE WHO ART KHEPHRA IN THY HIDING, EVEN UNTO THEE WHO ART KHEPH-RA IN THY SILENCE, WHO TRAVELEST OVER THE HEAVENS IN THY BARK AT THE MID-NIGHT HOUR OF THE SUN. TAHUTI STAND-ETH IN HIS SPLENDOR AT THE PROW, AND RA-HOOR ABIDETH AT THE HELM. HAIL UNTO THEE FROM THE ABODES OF EVENING!

Every single one of these adorations should be followed by the following affirmation:

Unity uttermost showed!
I adore the might of Thy breath,
Supreme and terrible God,
Who makest the gods and death
To tremble before Thee:—
I, I adore thee!

Appear on the throne of Ra!
Open the ways of the Khu!
Lighten the ways of the Ka!
The ways of the Khabs run through
To stir me or still me!
Aum! let it fill me!

The light is mine; its rays consume

Me: I have made a secret door
Into the House of Ra and Tum,
Of Khephra and of Ahathor.
I am thy Theban, O Mentu,
The Prophet Ankh-af-na-khonsu!

By Bes-na-Maut my breast I beat;
By wise Ta-Nech I weave my spell.
Show thy star-splendour, O Nuit!
Bid me within thine House to dwell,
O winged snake of light, Hadit!
Abide with me, Ra-Hoor-Khuit!

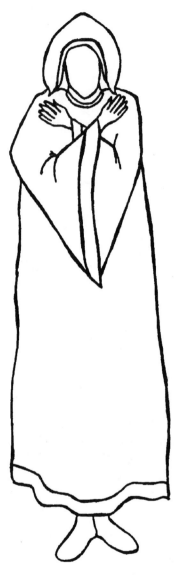

Sign of the Blazing Star
(East—Dawn)

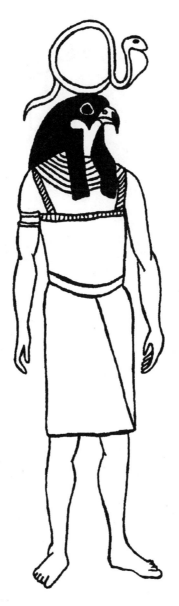

Egyptian God Ra
(East—Dawn)

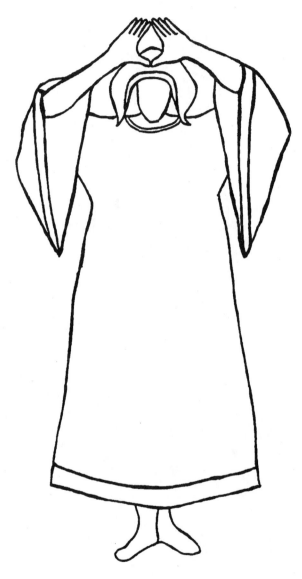

The Sign of Fire
(South—Noon)

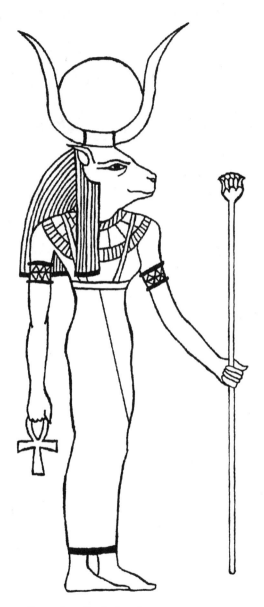

Egyptian God Ahathoor
(South—Noon)

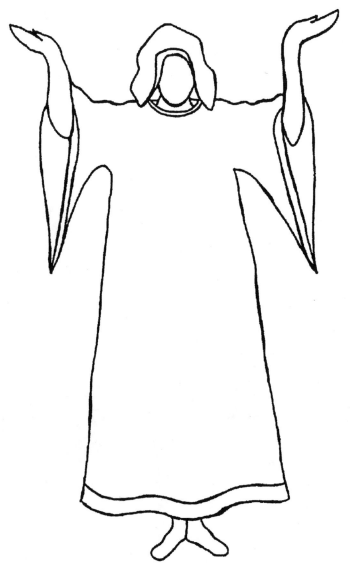

The Sign of the Egyptian God Shu Supporting the Sky
(West—Sunset)

Egyptian God Tum
(West—Sunset)

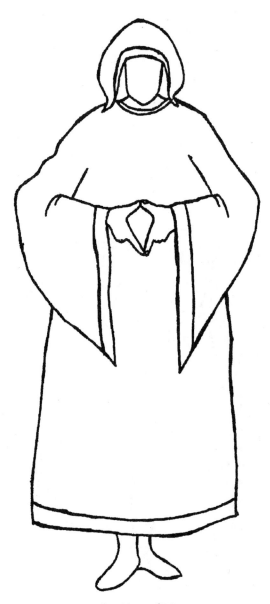

The Sign of Water
(North—Midnight)

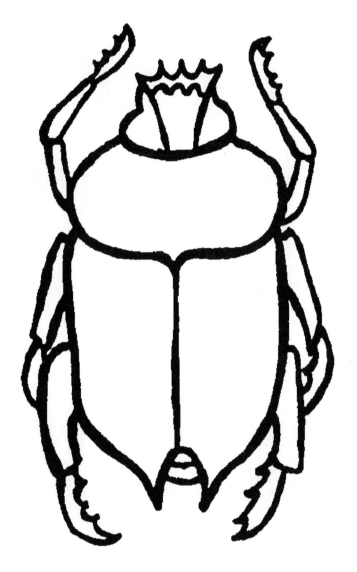

Egyptian God Khephra
(North—Midnight)

Correspondences

Hebrew Letter	English Equivalent	Meaning	Path No.	Letter Value	Tarot Attribution	Astrological, Planetary, or Elemental Correspondence
א Aleph	A	Ox	11	1	The Fool	Air △
ב Beth	B	House	12	2	Magician	Mercury ☿
ג Gimel	G	Camel	13	3	Priestess	Luna ☽
ד Daleth	D	Door	14	4	Empress	Venus ♀
ה Heh	H	Window	15	5	The Star	Aquarius ♒
ו Vav	V, W	Nail	16	6	Hierophant	Taurus ♉
ז Zayin	Z	Sword	17	7	The Lovers	Gemini ♊
ח Cheth	Ch	Fence	18	8	Chariot	Cancer ♋
ט Teth	T	Serpent	19	9	Strength	Leo ♌
י Yod	Y	Open Hand	20	10	Hermit	Virgo ♍
כ Kaph	K	Fist	21	20, 500	The Wheel	Jupiter ♃

Correspondences (*continued*)

Hebrew Letter	English Equivalent	Meaning	Path No.	Letter Value	Tarot Attribution	Astrological, Planetary, or Elemental Correspondence
ל Lamed	L	Ox Goad	22	30	Justice	Libra ♎
מ Mem	M	Water	23	40, 600	Hanged Man	Water ▽
נ Nun	N	Fish	24	50, 700	Death	Scorpio ♏
ס Samech	S	Prop	25	60	Temperance	Sagittarius ♐
ע Ayin	O	Eye	26	70	The Devil	Capricorn ♑
פ Peh	P	Mouth	27	80, 800	The Tower	Mars ♂
צ Tzaddi	Tz	Fishhook	28	90, 900	Emperor	Aries ♈
ק Qoph	Q	Head	29	100	The Moon	Pisces ♓
ר Resh	R	Forehead	30	200	The Sun	Sol ☉
ש Shin	Sh	Tooth	31	300	Judgment	Fire △
ת Taw	T, Th	A Mark	32	400	The World	Saturn ♄

Elemental Correspondences

△	Fire	Heat and Dryness	Radiant Energy
▽	Water	Cold and Moisture	Fluids
△̶	Air	Heat and Moisture	Gases
▽̶	Earth	Cold and Dryness	Solids

Astrological Correspondences

Opposites		Zodiacal Triplicities	Planetary Triplicities
♈	♎	△ = ♈ ♌ ♐	△ = ♂ ☉ ♃
♉	♏	▽ = ♋ ♏ ♓	▽ = ☽ ♆ ♃
♊	♐	△̶ = ♊ ♎ ♒	△̶ = ☿ ♀ ♅ ♄
♋	♑	▽̶ = ♉ ♍ ♑	▽̶ = ♀ ☿ ♄
♌	♒		
♍	♓		

Astrological Correspondences *(continued)*

Exaltations	Planetary Rulership			
♅ is exalted in ♏	Saturn	♄	rules ♑ and ♒	
♄ is exalted in ♎	Jupiter	♃	rules ♐ and ♓	
♃ is exalted in ♋	Mars	♂	rules ♈ and ♏	
♂ is exalted in ♑	Sol	☉	rules ♌	
☉ is exalted in ♈	Venus	♀	rules ♉ and ♎	
♀ is exalted in ♓	Mercury	☿	rules ♐ and ♓	
☿ is exalted in ♍	Luna	☽	rules ♋	
♆ is exalted in ♌	Uranus	♅	—	
☽ is exalted in ♉	Neptune	♆	—	

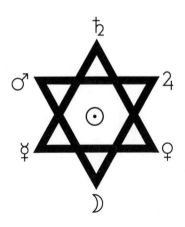

Curriculum:
Preliminaries

1. After about one month of practice in the Lesser Banishing Ritual of the Pentagram and Pranayama, choose for yourself a Magical Motto. This aspirational name may be phrased in Hebrew, Latin, Greek, Enochian, or any other language including English. Find one that qabalistically describes your inner nature best.

If after about a year you feel that you must change your motto as a result of your knowledge having been increased, do so. But wait at least a year. Record your name in your Magical Diary and use it whenever you use ritual.

2. Acquire your Robe, Altar, and elemental weapons. If it is within your talents, you may prefer to make your own implements. Magical items which are made by the person who uses them are much more powerful in the hands of the magician. When you manufacture these things, you focus a great deal of attention on the detail of the item being worked on. All data pertaining to the feel, weight, consistency, and temperature of the implement is being fed into the subconscious of the magician with very little effort on your part. All of this energy is absorbed into the implement; it then becomes an extension of your consciousness.

3. Design a ritual to declare to the Forces of the Universe your intention to embark on the adventure of self awareness. As with any magical operation, prepare the item to be purified and consecrated (in this case, your physical body) and the temple; see to it that they are both clean.

   Bathe your body and banish the temple using the Lesser Banishing Ritual of the Pentagram or the equivalent; burn incense therein. Write your aspiration on a piece of paper and burn it in a silver plate at your Altar at the end of the ceremony. Bury the ashes near an oak tree, and say: "This mighty tree will be a symbol of my devotion and dedication to the Great Work. As it weathers the rains, drought, hunger, and even time itself, so will I weather the demons which will tempt me to sway from the path I have chosen. To the glory of your ineffable name, AUM." Remember to always start the Work with a banishing.

4. Write a history of your existence. Write it in the third person, in other words: as if you were writing about someone else; it's a very effective method to remain objective.

Concentrate your efforts on the things that dramatically changed the course of your life, the things that made you the type of person that you are. Leave nothing significant unwritten. The more painful the experience, the stronger the impact it would have had on your life. By analyzing certain events it may become possible to discover where you are headed. This will bring you the knowledge of your True Will.

Once you feel that you have finished with your biography, it is an excellent practice to continue as though you were writing a "story." Continue until you are finished with the person's life. Create an adventure using the data and circumstances which life has given you this far, but always indicate in the manuscript when you started the "manipulation" by using a different color ink or ribbon, for example. This practice will divulge some of your deeper thoughts concerning your understanding of your True Will.

5. Write down all of the aspects of your everyday life on a piece of paper. Reveal everything; after all, no one will see it but you. Put a mark next to all of the things in which you have difficulty feeling spiritual; be honest. Study the reasons behind the lack of godliness in those actions, and work on them by using invocation, poetry, mantra, or some other form of devotion until you perceive every act in your daily routine as an act of worship to your God.

   If you came from a strict Christian upbringing you might find yourself questioning your sexuality, but remember: in the eyes of the consecrated everything is holy.

6. Remember to write *everything* you did in your Diary; if for some reason you want to reproduce the experi-

ence it will be necessary that you duplicate all of the events. The importance of a Diary cannot be overstressed. Magick is a science; keep notes on your experiments. (See "The Diary," page 132.)

7. Memorize correspondences.

8. Write a short study on each of the popular religions. Concentrate on the myth, and what it demands from its followers. When you are finished, compare notes and see what they have in common; but most importantly, record how you respond or react to each dogma and why.

9. Learn and practice Liber Resh or an equivalent adoration to the Highest.

10. Practice "Pranayama."

11. Practice and gain control over your astral body.

This may seem like a lot of work; it is. But I assure you, as you accustom yourself to this routine, you will employ muscles in your brain that may have been long forgotten. These exercises will stimulate parts of your brain which in most people have lain dormant since childhood. If you are serious about magick, you have everything to gain and nothing to lose from the activities listed above.

Contact Lists

Magical Organizations

A∴A∴ c/o College of Thelema
P.O. Box 415
Oroville, CA 95965

A∴A∴ c/o Temple of Thelema
222 N. Manhattan Pl.
Los Angeles, CA 90007

College of Thelema
P.O. Box 415
Oroville, CA 95965

Ordo Templi Orientis
JAF Box 7666
New York, NY 10116

Temple of Thelema
222 N. Manhattan Pl.
Los Angeles, CA 90007

Fraternitas LVX Occulta
P.O. Box 5094
Covina, CA 91723

Suppliers of Incenses, Oils, and Related Materials

Ananda Books
3663 Canyon Crest Dr.
Riverside, CA 92507

Arts of Sorcery
577 5th St.
Oakland, CA 94607

Bodhi Tree
8585 Melrose Ave.
Los Angeles, CA 90069

Ceridwen's
461 N. Western Ave.
Los Angeles, CA 90004

Eye of the Cat
3314 E. Broadway
Long Beach, CA 90803

House Of Hermetics
2146 W. Colorado Blvd.
Eagle Rock, CA 90041

Lady Bountiful
1513 Aviation Blvd
Redondo Beach, CA 90278

Lady Nuit Distributions
438 De Chanbly
Laval, Quebec H7W 4K1
CANADA

Magickal Childe
35 W. 19th St.
New York, NY 10011

Magick Store
2306 Highland Ave.
National City, CA 92050

Mermade
5952 Appian Way
Long Beach, CA 90803

Magick Circle
956 N. Lake
Pasadena, CA 91104

New Leaf
5425 Tulane Dr. SW
Atlanta, GA 30336

Nuit Unlimited Imports
249 N. Brand Blvd # 482
Glendale, CA 91203

Panurge Emporium
1005 NW 16th
Portland, OR 97209
(503) 248-6905

Psychic Eye
1345 Ventura Blvd.
Sherman Oaks, CA 91423

Serpents Occult
PO Box 290644
Port Orange, FL 32129

Sorcerer Shop
8246 1/2 Santa Monica Blvd.
Los Angeles, CA 90046

White Light Pentacle
PO Box 8163
Salem, MA 01971

Robes, Bags,
Pouches, and Other Textiles

Leo Nine
P.O. Box 9053
Portland, OR 97207

STAY IN TOUCH

On the following pages you will find some of the books now available on related subjects. Your book dealer stocks most of these and will stock new titles in the Llewellyn series as they become available. We urge your patronage.

To obtain our full catalog, to keep informed about new titles as they are released and to benefit from informative articles and helpful news, you are invited to write for our bimonthly news magazine/catalog, *Llewellyn's New Worlds of Mind and Spirit.* A sample copy is free, and it will continue coming to you at no cost as long as you are an active mail customer. Or you may subscribe for just $10.00 in the U.S.A. and Canada ($20.00 overseas, first class mail). Many bookstores also have *New Worlds* available to their customers. Ask for it.

Llewellyn's New Worlds of Mind and Spirit
P.O. Box 64383-213, St. Paul, MN 55164-0383, U.S.A.
* * *

TO ORDER BOOKS AND TAPES

If your book dealer does not have the books described, you may order them directly from the publisher by sending full price in U.S. funds, plus $3.00 for postage and handling for orders *under* $10.00; $4.00 for orders *over* $10.00. There are no postage and handling charges for orders over $50.00. Postage and handling rates are subject to change. We ship UPS whenever possible. Delivery guaranteed. Provide your street address as UPS does not deliver to P.O. Boxes. UPS to Canada requires a $50.00 minimum order. Allow 4-6 weeks for delivery. Orders outside the U.S.A. and Canada: Airmail—add retail price of book; add $5.00 for each non-book item (tapes, etc.); add $1.00 per item for surface mail.

FOR GROUP STUDY AND PURCHASE

Because there is a great deal of interest in group discussion and study of the subject matter of this book, we offer a special quantity price to group leaders or agents. Our Special Quantity Price for a minimum order of five copies of *New Aeon Magick* is $29.97 cash-with-order. This price includes postage and handling within the United States. Minnesota residents must add 6.5% sales tax. For additional quantities, please order in multiples of five. For Canadian and foreign orders, add postage and handling charges as above. Credit card (VISA, MasterCard, American Express) orders are accepted. Charge card orders only ($15.00 minimum order) may be phoned in free within the U.S.A. or Canada by dialing 1-800-THE-MOON. For customer service, call 1-612-291-1970. Mail orders to:

LLEWELLYN PUBLICATIONS
P.O. Box 64383-213, St. Paul, MN 55164-0383, U.S.A.

Prices subject to change without notice.

RITUAL MAGIC
What It Is & How To Do It
by Donald Tyson

For thousands of years men and women have practiced it despite the severe repression of sovereigns and priests. Now, *Ritual Magic* takes you into the heart of that entrancing, astonishing and at times mystifying secret garden of *magic*.

What is this ancient power? Where does it come from? How does it work? Is it mere myth and delusion, or can it truly move mountains and make the dead speak. . . bring rains from a clear sky and calm the seas. . . turn the outcome of great battles and call down the Moon from Heaven? Which part of the claims made for magic are true in the most literal sense, and which are poetic exaggerations that must be interpreted symbolically? How can magic be used to improve *your* life?

This book answers these and many other questions in a clear and direct manner. Its purpose is to separate the wheat from the chaff and make sense of the non-sense. It explains what the occult revival is all about, reveals the foundations of practical ritual magic, showing how modern occultism grew from a single root into a number of clearly defined esoteric schools and pagan sects.

0-87542-835-5, 288 pgs., 6 x 9, illus., index, softcover $12.95

MODERN MAGICK
Eleven Lessons in the High Magickal Arts
by Donald Michael Kraig

Modern Magick is the most comprehensive step-by-step introduction to the art of ceremonial magic ever offered. The eleven lessons in this book will guide you from the easiest of rituals and the construction of your magickal tools through the highest forms of magick: designing your own rituals and doing pathworking. Along the way you will learn the secrets of the Kabbalah in a clear and easy-to-understand manner. You will discover the true secrets of invocation (channeling) and evocation, and the missing information that will finally make the ancient grimoires, such as the "Keys of Solomon," not only comprehensible, but usable. This book also contains one of the most in-depth chapters on sex magick ever written. *Modern Magick* is designed so anyone can use it, and it is the perfect guidebook for students and classes. It will also help to round out the knowledge of long-time practitioners of the magickal arts.

0-87542-324-8, 592 pgs., 6 x 9, illus., index, softcover $14.95

Prices subject to change without notice.

MAGICIAN'S COMPANION
A Practical and Encyclopedic Guide to Magical and Religious Symbolism
by Bill Whitcomb
The Magician's Companion is a "desk reference" overflowing with a wide range of occult and esoteric materials absolutely indispensable to anyone engaged in the magickal arts!

The magical knowledge of our ancestors comprises an intricate and elegant technology of the mind and imagination. This book attempts to make the ancient systems accessible, understandable and useful to modern magicians by categorizing and cross-referencing the major magical symbol-systems (i.e., world views on inner and outer levels). Students of religion, mysticism, mythology, symbolic art, literature, and even cryptography will find this work of value.

This comprehensive book discusses and compares over 35 magical models (e.g., the Trinities, the Taoist Psychic Centers, Enochian magic, the qabala, the Worlds of the Hopi Indians). Also included are discussions of the theory and practice of magic and ritual; sections on alchemy, magical alphabets, talismans, sigils, magical herbs and plants; suggested programs of study; an extensive glossary and bibliography; and much more.

0-87542-868-1, 522 pgs., 7 x 10, illus., softcover   **$19.95**

PILGRIMS OF THE NIGHT
Pathfinders of the Magical Way
by Lars B. Lindholm
Here is a fresh, unprejudiced and exceptionally readable examination of the evolution of magical theory and practice in Western culture. In his often humorous style, Lars B. Lindholm traces the history of magic from the earliest times, beginning with prehistoric magic, Atlantis, Egypt, Greece and continuing through the Middle Ages, when the dissemination of magic was accelerated by the printing press and the merchant class's need for education. Encounter colorful personalities including Roger Bacon, Albertus Magnus, and Thomas Aquinas. After a look at the Rosicrucian phenomenon, you will meet Henry Cornelius Agrippa, John Dee, Francis Barrett, Eliphas Levi, and Madame Blavatsky. Explore the Golden Dawn and Aleister Crowley, and learn the truth about occultism and magic within Nazism. Finally, explore current phenomena, including chaos magic and the acolytes of H.P. Lovecraft's fictional scenarios. The appendix deals with the magical curriculum of the Golden Dawn, how magic works, the Tarot, and the astrological charts of some prominent personalities.

0-87542-474-0, 256 pgs., 6 x 9, illus., softbound   **$12.00**

Prices subject to change without notice.

THE KEY OF IT ALL
BOOK ONE: THE EASTERN MYSTERIES
An Encyclopedic Guide to the Sacred Languages & Magical Systems
of the World
by David Allen Hulse

The Key of It All series clarifies and extends the knowledge established by all previous books on occult magick. Book One catalogs and distills, in hundreds of tables of secret symbolism, the true alphabet magick of every ancient Eastern magickal tradition. Unlike the current rash of publications which do no more than recapitulate Regardie or Crowley, *The Key of It All* series establishes a new level of competence in all fields of magick both East and West.

Key 1: Cuneiform—the oldest tradition ascribing number to word; the symbolism of base 60 used in Babylonian and Sumerian Cuneiform; the first God and Goddess names associated to number.

Key 2: Hebrew—a complete exposition of the rules governing the Hebrew Qabalah; the evolution of the Tree of Life; an analysis of the *Book of Formation,* the oldest key to the symbolic meaning of the Hebrew alphabet.

Key 3: Arabic—the similarity between the Hebrew and Arabic Qabalahs; the secret Quranic symbolism for the Arabic alphabet; the Persian alphabet code; the philosophical numbering system of G.I. Gurdjieff.

Key 4: Sanskrit—the secret Vedic number codes for Sanskrit; the digital word-numbers; the symbolism of the seven chakras and their numerical key.

Key 5: Tibetan—the secret number lore for Tibetan as inspired by the Sanskrit codes; the secret symbols for the Tibetan alphabet; the six major schools of Tattva philosophy.

Key 6: Chinese—the Taoist calligraphic stroke count technique for number Chinese characters; Chinese Taoist number philosophy; the I Ching, the Japanese language and its parallels to the Chinese number system.

0-87542-318-3, 592 pgs., 7 x 10, tables, charts, softcover $19.95

THE KEY OF IT ALL
BOOK TWO: THE WESTERN MYSTERIES
An Encyclopedic Guide to the Sacred Languages & Magical Systems
of the World
by David Allen Hulse

The Key of It All series clarifies and extends the knowledge established by all
previous books on occult magick. Book Two catalogs and distills, in hundreds of tables of secret symbolism, the true alphabet magick of every
ancient Western magickal tradition. Unlike the current rash of publications
which do no more than recapitulate Regardie or Crowley, *The Key of It All*
series establishes a new level of competence in all fields of magick both East
and West.

Key 7: Greek—the number codes for Greek; the Gnostic cosmology; the
Pythagorean philosophical metaphors for the number series.

Key 8: Coptic—the number values for Coptic, derived from the Greek;
Coptic astrological symbolism; the Egyptian hieroglyphs and their influence in the numbering of Hebrew and Greek.

Key 9: Runes—the ancient runic alphabet codes for Germanic, Icelandic,
Scandinavian, and English Rune systems; the modern German Armanen
Runic cult; the Irish Ogham and Beth-Luis-Nion poetic alphabets.

Key 10: Latin—Roman Numerals as the first Latin code; the Lullian Latin
Qabalah; the Germanic and Italian serial codes for Latin; the Renaissance
cosmological model of three worlds.

Key 11: Enochian—the number codes for Enochian according to John Dee,
S.L. MacGregor Mathers, and Aleister Crowley; the true pattern behind the
Watchtower symbolism; the complete rectified Golden Dawn correspon-
dences for the Enochian alphabet.

Key 12: Tarot—the pictorial key to the Hebrew alphabet; the divinatory
system for the Tarot; the two major Qabalistic codes for the Tarot emanat-
ing from France and England.

Key 13: English—the seria l order code for English; Aleister Crowley's
attempt of an English Qabalah; the symbolism behind the shapes of the
English alphabet letters.

0-87542-379-5, 592 pgs., 7 x 10, tables, charts, softcover $19.95

THE THREE BOOKS OF OCCULT PHILOSOPHY
Completely Annotated, with Modern Commentary—The Foundation
Book of Western Occultism
by Henry Cornelius Agrippa, edited and annotated by Donald Tyson
Agrippa's *Three Books of Occult Philosophy* is the single most important text
in the history of Western occultism. Occultists have drawn upon it for five
centuries, although they rarely give it credit. First published in Latin in 1531
and translated into English in 1651, it has never been reprinted in its
entirety since. Photocopies are hard to find and very expensive. Now, for
the first time in 500 years, *Three Books of Occult Philosophy* will be presented
as Agrippa intended. There were many errors in the original translation,
but occult author Donald Tyson has made the corrections and has clarified
the more obscure material with copious notes.

This is a necessary reference tool not only for all magicians, but also for
scholars of the Renaissance, Neoplatonism, the Western Kabbalah, the history of ideas and sciences and the occult tradition. It is as practical today as
it was 500 years ago.

0-87542-832-0, 1,080 pgs., 7 x 10, softcover $29.95

GOLDEN DAWN ENOCHIAN MAGIC
by Pat Zalewski
Enochian magic is considered by most magicians to be the most powerful
system ever created. Aleister Crowley learned this system of magic from the
Hermetic Order of the Golden Dawn, which had developed and expanded
the concepts and discoveries of Elizabethan magus John Dee. This book
picks up where the published versions of the Enochian material of the
Golden Dawn leave off.

Based on the research and unpublished papers of MacGregor Mathers, one
of the founders of the Golden Dawn, *Golden Dawn Enochian Magic* opens
new avenues of use for this system. New insights are given on such topics as
the Sigillum Dei Aemeth, the Angels of the Enochian Aires applied to the 12
tribes of Israel and the Kabbalah, the 91 Governors, the Elemental Tablets
as applied to the celestial sphere, and more. This book provides a long-
sought break from amateurish and inaccurate books on the subject; it is
designed to complement such scholarly classics as *Enochian Invocation* and
Heptarchia Mystica.

0-87542-898-3, 224 pgs., 5 1/4 x 8, illus., softcover $12.95

Prices subject to change without notice.